Aligning IEPs
to the Common Core State Standards

**for Students with Moderate
and Severe Disabilities**

Ginevra Courtade, PhD
Diane M. Browder, PhD

**Updated
Version with
Common Core
State Standards**

IEP

RESOURCES

Authors: Ginevra Courtade, PhD, and Diane M. Browder, PhD
Editors: Tom Kinney and Joan Donovan
Graphic Design: Sherry Pribbenow

An Attainment Publication

Attainment Company, Inc.
P.O. Box 930160
Verona, Wisconsin 53593-0160 USA
1-800-327-4269
www.AttainmentCompany.com

ISBN 1-57861-548-8

Contents

About the Authors

Ginevra R. Courtade, PhD

Dr. Ginevra Courtade is an assistant professor in special education at the University of Louisville in Kentucky. Dr. Courtade has worked in the field of moderate/severe disabilities for over 10 years. She has been a classroom teacher, a grant-funded project trainer, a research associate, and now trains teachers and conducts research at the university level. Her work focuses specifically on teaching academics to students with moderate/severe disabilities and preparing teachers to instruct students using the general education curriculum. She has numerous publications to her credit, including journal articles, book chapters, the Early Literacy Skills Builder, and Teaching to Standards: Science.

Dr. Courtade received her bachelor's degree in psychology from the State University of New York at Buffalo, her master's degree in special education from D'Youville College, and her doctoral degree in special education from the University of North Carolina-Charlotte. She taught students with moderate/severe disabilities in the Charlotte-Mecklenburg Schools and was a grant liaison between UNCC and CMS before taking on the role of research associate at UNCC. Prior to her current position, Dr. Courtade spent two years at West Virginia University, where she served as an assistant professor in special education.

Currently, Dr. Courtade works closely with the Kentucky Department of Education to provide training and support to new teachers of students with moderate and severe disabilities. She also trains teachers nationally to implement academic curricula for their students.

The authors wish to thank Jean Vintinner, Instructor of Reading from University of North Carolina at Charlotte for her review of the alignment of the ELA objectives and Karen Karp, Professor of Mathematics Education from the University of Louisville for her review of the alignment of the mathematics objectives.

Diane M. Browder, PhD

Dr. Diane Browder is the Lake and Edward P. Snyder Distinguished Professor of Special Education at the University of North Carolina at Charlotte. Dr. Browder has over two decades of research and writing on assessment and instruction for students with severe developmental disabilities including textbooks, curricula, and numerous journal publications. Her work focuses on teaching general curriculum content (reading, mathematics, and science) and alternate assessment based on alternate achievement standards. She has been Principal Investigator for several grants on access to general curriculum, including two recent IES-funded research projects—one on early literacy and the other on math and science for students with significant cognitive disabilities. She also is a partner in the OSEP-funded National Center and State Collaborative focused on alternate assessment.

Dr. Diane Browder received her bachelor's degree in psychology from Duke University and her master's and doctoral degrees in special education from the University of Virginia. In her early career, she was a recreational therapist at Duke Hospital and a cross-categorical special education teacher in Nelson County, Virginia. Dr. Browder spent 17 years at Lehigh University in Bethlehem, Pennsylvania, where she served as professor and coordinator of special education. While at Lehigh, Dr. Browder developed a model program for children with autism, community services for adults with severe disabilities, and supported employment for individuals with a wide range of disabilities. In 1998, Dr. Browder accepted the distinguished professorship at the University of North Carolina at Charlotte. In her 12 years at UNC Charlotte, Dr. Browder has worked closely with the Charlotte Mecklenburg School System and a team of researchers to develop new interventions and curricula in literacy, science, mathematics, and social studies. She also has been involved in developing alignment strategies for state's alternate assessment systems.

In 2009, Dr. Browder received the Distinguished Researcher Award from the AERA Special Education SIG and was the First Citizens Bank Scholar at the University of North Carolina at Charlotte. Dr. Browder also has received national and state awards for her service to individuals with disabilities. In 2011 she was awarded the O. Max Gardner Award for the faculty member in North Carolina whose research has had the greatest impact on the human race.

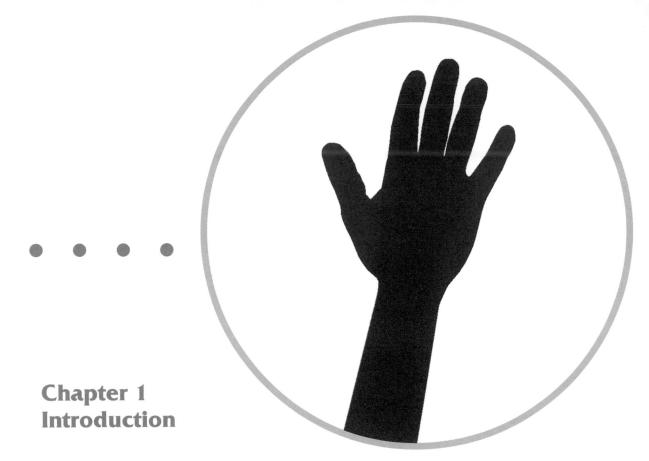

Chapter 1
Introduction

What Does Alignment to Academic Standards Mean?

Angela has a standards-based IEP that is based on the Common Core State Standards which her state adopted to define the knowledge and skills all students should have within their K-12 education careers in mathematics and language arts. Her IEP also aligns with her state's standards in science and social studies. Angela demonstrates her achievement through the state's alternate assessment. Angela also helps her teacher track her progress for some priority academic skills. For example, she uses an object chart to keep track of how many books she has completed through shared readings. In addition to the core academic content Angela learns, she also continues to work on personal care, therapy, and social goals which she developed with her IEP team. Angela's local community college has a new program to support and include students with moderate and severe intellectual disabilities. Although Angela is only in the 7th grade, she and her class have visited the program and talked about skills needed to be ready for college and a future career.

Developing standards-based IEPs for students with moderate and severe disabilities is an evolving process. In the late 1990s, educators began to respond to the requirements of IDEA (1997) to promote access to the general curriculum and to include all students in state and district assessments. Some students needed alternate assessments because they could not participate in large-scale assessments with accommodations. Although alternate assessments have changed in the last 20 years and are likely to continue to evolve, providing students with the opportunity to learn general curriculum content is an ongoing priority. An important way that IEPs promote learning in the general curriculum is through alignment with state standards. Since 2010, many states have adopted the Common Core State Standards. The Common Core State Standards define the knowledge and skills that students are to learn in their K-12 education (www.corestandards.org). Let's begin by defining some of the terms you will see throughout this book.

What is the General Curriculum?

The general curriculum includes the full educational experience available to all students. General curriculum **content** includes the subjects that all students study, including both core academic areas and subjects like art, music, physical and career education. In this book, we will focus on the core academic content areas of mathematics, language arts, science, and social studies. States have standards for what students will learn in these core content areas. The general curriculum **context** is the general education classroom and other school environments where students receive instruction.

What are Standards?

Standards provide statements of outcomes all learners should achieve. Through the use of general assessments (e.g., a 4th grade reading test), schools determine if students are meeting the expected targets for their grade level. Schools are accountable for students meeting these achievement targets, that is, for making adequate yearly progress. Standards are usually arranged by grade level and content area. For example, if you look at the Common Core State Standards (www.corestandards.org), you can look up a content area (e.g., mathematics) and then the expectations for a grade level (e.g., 7th grade). At the time this book was written, there were standards developed in Mathematics and English Language Arts. Most states have adopted these common core standards, but also have additional standards in other content areas like science and social studies.

Students with disabilities learn these same standards for their grade level placement. A student with a disability in the 8th grade will focus on the 8th grade standards. For the student to be successful, educators need to plan for the use of instructional supports, accommodations, and assistive technology. Students who cannot participate in the general assessment and take an alternate assessment may focus on some priorities within these core standards. These may be provided by the state in a special curricular planning resource for students who take alternate assessment. These prioritizations are sometimes called curricular frameworks or extended standards, or simply "extensions."

Here is an example of a Common Core State Standard in Writing for 4th Grade:[1]

Write narratives to develop real or imagined experiences or events using effective techniques, descriptive details, and clear event sequences.

a. *Orient the reader by establishing a situation and introducing a narrator and/or characters; organize an event sequence that unfolds naturally.*

b. *Use dialogue and description to develop experiences and events or show the responses of characters to situations.*

c. *Use a variety of transitional words and phrases to manage the sequence of events.*

d. *Use concrete words and phrases and sensory details to convey experiences and events precisely.*

e. *Provide a conclusion that follows from the narrated experiences or events.*

---

[1] http://www.corestandards.org/the-standards/english-language-arts-standards/writing/grade-4/

Students with disabilities can be taught to write a narrative with all five characteristics using assistive technology, instructional supports, and accommodations (e.g., dictate to scribe). For example, as an accommodation, some students with severe disabilities may need to dictate the passage to a scribe. That is, they may be able to compose it, but not have the mechanics of writing. Some students may also need the support of sentence strips, pictures with captions, or objects to help create this dictation. Some may be able to use software that creates the word when a picture is selected. An extended standard for 5th graders taking alternate assessment based on alternate achievement standards might focus on some components of the narrative and alternatives like using dictation to scribe. For example, an extended standard might be:

> Take a few minutes to look up both the Common Core State Standards and what your state's education website contains on standards. Can you find any information on extended standards? (You may find it under Alternate Assessment.)

Write narratives that summarize familiar experiences (e.g., coming to school, going to grocery store) that include the situation, characters, a sequence of three events, and a conclusion. Writing may be completed using assistive technology and supports such as sentence strips, pictures, and objects with captions.

What is a Standards-Based IEP?

An IEP, or individualized education plan, is a requirement of IDEA (2004)[2] and specifies the special education services a student with disabilities will receive. The IEP for students who participate in alternate assessment based on alternate achievement standards includes: (a) a statement of the present level of performance in both academic achievement and functional performance, (b) a statement of measurable annual goals (both academic and functional), (c) a description of benchmarks or short-term objectives, (d) a description of how student progress towards the goals will be measured, (e) a statement regarding related services and supplementary aids and services (based on peer-reviewed research) to be provided, (f) an explanation of the extent to which the student will not participate in the general education classroom, (g) a statement of any accommodations needed to measure academic and functional achievement of the student, (h) frequency, location, and duration of services, and (i) postsecondary goals beginning when the student is 16 years old. The main difference

[2] Individuals with Disabilities Education Improvement Act of 2004, 20 U. S. C. §1400, H. R. 1350.

in the IEP requirements for students who participate in alternate assessment aligned to alternate achievement standards is the inclusion of benchmarks or short-term objectives.

Educators have been creating IEPs since the first federal law for students with disabilities was passed in 1975. A newer concept is the standards-based IEP. A standards-based IEP includes goals that promote learning of the state standards. It does not try to include a goal for every state standard in every content area. This would result in a very long document! Instead, it provides goals for the strategies students need to develop to learn the general curriculum content. Sometimes, the goals help focus priorities within the general curriculum content for students who take the alternate assessment.

What is Alternate Assessment?

Students who are not able to take the general state assessments with or without accommodations are provided an alternate assessment. This alternate assessment is developed by the state and administered with students who are identified by their IEP teams as needing this option. In some states, educators collect a portfolio of products to document student progress. In other states, educators administer an assessment with performance tasks students complete, or use a checklist summary of achievement. Some states use a hybrid of these methods. Whatever method the state selects, educators follow state guidelines for the administration of the assessment. This book focuses on students who will take an alternate assessment based on alternate achievement standards, an option abbreviated as AA-AAS.

Who are Students with Severe Disabilities?

As described under "What are Standards?" students in AA-AAS may be working on extensions of the state standards. When No Child Left Behind (2002)[3] was passed, states could count up to 1% of students participating in the assessment system as proficient using alternate assessments based on alternate achievement standards. For this reason, students who participate in AA-AAS are sometimes referred to as "the 1%." Federal policy refers to students who take AA-AAS as having "significant cognitive disabilities." Each state sets eligibility criteria, but these criteria cannot be based on the disability label (e.g., having a severe intellectual disability does not automatically qualify the student to take AA-AAS). Although students who take AA-

[3] No Child Left Behind Act of 2001, Pub. L. No. 107-110, 118 Stat.1425 (2002).

AAS may include students from any disability category who have more severe levels of the disability, this book focuses especially on students who have a moderate or severe intellectual disability. This intellectual disability may accompany other disabilities such as autism, sensory, or physical impairments. We chose to use the term "intellectual disability" rather "cognitive disability" because the term is recognized broadly by professional organizations and under Rosa's Law,[4] a federal law signed in 2010 that will change references in federal law from *mental retardation* to *intellectual disability*, and references to a *mentally retarded individual* to an *individual with an intellectual disability*. For shorthand, we will use the term "moderate and severe disability" to refer to students with intellectual functioning that is at least moderately impaired and who may also have multiple disabilities.

What is Alignment?

Alignment is the process of matching two educational components, which then strengthens the purpose and goals of both. For example, instruction can be aligned with assessment; assessment can be aligned with state standards; and IEPs can be aligned with state standards to help align instruction with the general curriculum. Before considering alignment in more detail, it is helpful to consider three reasons why alignment is important.

1. IEPs aligned with state standards can prepare students for state assessments.

To meet alternate achievement standards, students need instruction that is aligned with the academic content standards for their grade. The IEP is not meant to restate all of these content standards, but should specify skills for the student to acquire that will promote access to this curriculum and help the student meet the alternate achievement standards. State standards can seem overwhelming to the classroom teacher and other educators. The IEP helps the team know the priorities for addressing these standards.

2. For students to show progress in academic content, they need academic instruction.

In the past, educators sometimes taught functional or life skills curriculum as a replacement for the general curriculum. Life skills are important for increased independence and transition to adult living, but students also need the opportunity to participate in the general curriculum for their grade level. Young students especially need the opportunity to gain skills in literacy and math. Sometimes in the

[4] http://www.govtrack.us/congress/bill.xpd?bill=s111-2781

past students with moderate and severe disabilities received little or no academic instruction. Because students with moderate and severe disabilities need direct and systematic instruction, they are not likely to learn academic skills unless they receive this instruction.

The IEP is not intended to define all of this instruction, nor does it function as the student's curriculum. Instead, it points the way for you to set priorities for what the student will master and how s/he will access the broader content.

3. Well-aligned IEPs can promote meaningful academic instruction.

Deciding what academic skills to teach students with moderate and severe disabilities can be difficult. Sometimes the goal that is chosen does not appear to be "really reading" or "really math" when presented to general educators. Sometimes it is clearly academic, but with little real-life use or meaning for the student. Sometimes it is academic, but not relevant to the student's current grade level content. Knowing how to align an IEP to state standards can help planning teams select academic goals that are meaningful for the student and promote access to the general curriculum.

Further Understanding Alignment

Alignment occurs when there is a match between the written, taught, and tested curriculum. The alignment of these educational components can be illustrated as follows:

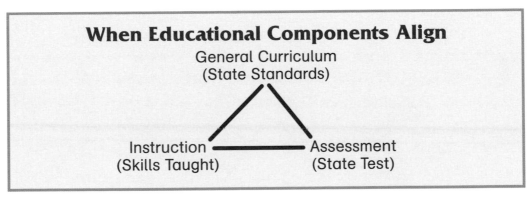

Notice that the instruction addresses content to be covered by the state test and links to the state standards.

The IEP can help define priorities for student mastery within this curriculum as well as skills students can use to access grade-level content. When a student has an IEP, well-aligned educational components can be illustrated in this way:

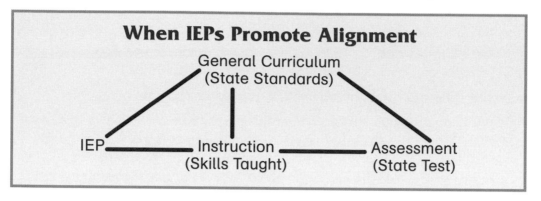

Note that the IEP helps focus the instruction.

To see what the pattern looks like when IEPs don't align, consider a hypothetical general education context in which educational components are aligned. For example, Ms. Jones is teaching her third grade class to multiply using numbers 1-12.

Her state's 3rd grade mathematics standards include beginning multiplication. The state's 3rd grade math assessment will measure how well her students multiply. In this example, the taught curriculum aligns well with both the written curriculum (state standards) and tested curriculum (state test). The alignment can be diagrammed like this:

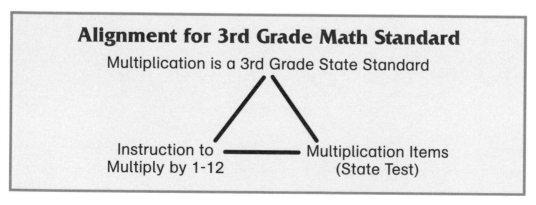

Ms. Smith is the special educator for 3rd grade students with moderate and severe disabilities. Her students participate in the state's alternate assessment. One portion of the assessment determines if students can group items and count the sets (concrete form of multiplication). The only math skill Ms. Smith has targeted for student IEPs is telling time. In the following example, students do not have instruction aligned to state standards:

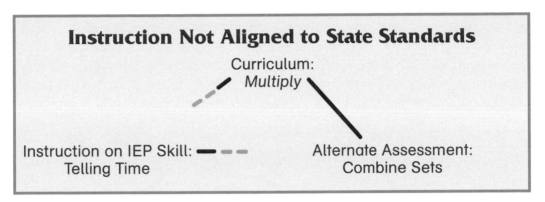

To her credit, after learning more about alignment to state standards and considering her students' skills, Ms. Smith decides to add instruction on combining sets for her 3rd grade class. Ms. Smith presents this as an early vocational task in creating supplies packets at a job site. For example, the teacher has them make three sets of art supplies with two pens in each set. Or, they create bags for the homeless shelter with three items in eight bags. They then find out how many items they have used in all. To help her students understand, Ms. Smith uses pictures of the task with numbers and the mathematical signs "x" and "=". She works with Ms. Jones, the general education teacher, so all students can have the option of using a wider range of manipulatives for the multiplication lessons. The students with disabilities work with peers to check their multiplication worksheets by creating sets of items. Ms. Smith now has instruction that aligns as follows:

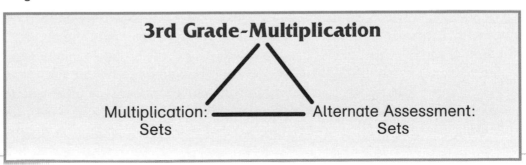

When planning for John's 3rd grade year, Ms. Smith is aware that he's challenged in learning to combine sets because he has only limited use of one hand. He makes most of his responses through the use of his voice output picture communication AAC device, or through using a switch that functions as a mouse for the computer. Currently, he only uses the switch to activate cause-and-effect software games. To master the concept of combining sets, John needs to learn how to first create and then count sets. So the team decides that one IEP goal will be for John to learn to use the first portion of a math software program that introduces multiplication by showing pictures of arrays of items. John also needs to learn to identify numbers with his AAC device. For example, when the teacher says "nine," John can locate "9" on his device. This goal will provide broader access to numerous math activities in 3rd grade. Here is how his IEP promotes alignment of his instruction to the 3rd grade math standards:

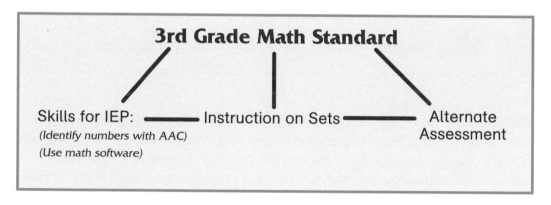

Alignment with high school curriculum can be especially challenging when the gap between the general curriculum and students' current academic skills is large. For example, state standards for 10th grade English target understanding symbolism in poetry and other literature. Here the IEP team is planning for Ramona, a student with severe disabilities who currently has no reading skills but enjoys the social context of being with typical peers in English class. The IEP team wants to build on Ramona's social success by promoting some literacy skills that link to the poetry focus of 10th grade. Since Ramona has used picture symbols for basic needs and social communication, the IEP team considers how she might learn the more abstract symbols of poetry. Similarly, the team considers the state standards in other academic areas like math and science. Because of Ramona's age, the team also wants to target some life skills like learning to follow picture/word directions to complete a vocational task. The following diagram shows how the team uses the IEP to focus on both life skills and general curriculum. While this state's alternate assessment only targets academic skills, Ramona's progress in learning life skills is also important for her transition planning.

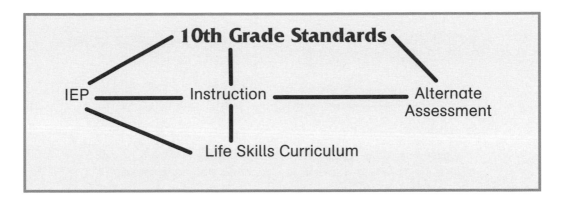

Selecting IEP Goals to Promote Alignment

Once the concept of alignment is clear, it's helpful to consider guidelines for developing an IEP that includes goals that align to state standards. The product that results from this process is a standards-based IEP. These guidelines require learning more about the general curriculum as outlined in the state standards and determining how to create access to it for your students with moderate and severe disabilities.

Guideline One:
Become Familiar with State Standards

The IEP team first needs to become familiar with state standards for the student's assigned grade level. For most states, these will incorporate the Common Core State Standards for mathematics and English Language Arts. The "assigned" grade level, usually based on chronological age, typically differs from the instructional grade level for students with moderate and severe disabilities. For example, a student who is 7 years old will probably be assigned to 2nd grade. In contrast, her "instructional" grade level may

> The "assigned" grade level is usually based on chronological age, which for students with moderate and severe disabilities typically differs from the instructional grade level.

be at a beginning point of academic learning, and may not correspond to a specific grade level designation. In focusing on alignment, the educational team considers how to create access to the student's assigned grade level (e.g., 2nd grade) while also using information on present level of performance (instructional level), to pinpoint objectives for academic learning. The following figure illustrates this concept.

Develop Alignment Based on Assigned Grade Level for General Curriculum Access

Assigned Grade Level:

2nd Grade ➞ 2nd Grade State Standards

Instructional Level: Entry Level Academic Skills (below K-1)

Align to 2nd Grade, not Kindergarten, for age-appropriate general curriculum access for students with moderate and severe disabilities.

Information on state standards is typically available on each state's education agency website. This information may provide a deeper understanding of the standard and how to address this concept instructionally. Table 1.1 provides an example adapted from the Massachusetts Department of Education that includes the state standard, the essence of the standard, and instructional ideas.

Since 2010, most states have adopted the Common Core State Standards in English Language Arts and Mathematics.

Table 1.1	**Strand: Earth and Space Science** **Topic: Earth in the Solar System**[5] **Grade Level 6-8**
Learning Standard as Written	Recognize that gravity is a force that pulls all things on and near the earth toward the center of the earth. Gravity plays a major role in the formation of the planets, stars, and solar system, and in determining their motions. (Standard 8)
Essence of the Standard	Gravity is a force. The effects of the earth's gravitational pull and the motion of objects in the solar system.
Instructional Idea	At grades 6-8 (or an equivalent age), students observe the speed at which objects of various mass fall from the same height. Using a chronometer to accurately measure time, they plot the data as "mass versus time."

[5] Examples abstracted from the Resource Guide to the Massachusetts Curriculum Frameworks for Students with Disabilities: Science and Technology/Engineering published by the Massachusetts Department of Education http://www.doe.mass.edu/mcas/alt/rg/sci.pdf pp. 260-261.

Table 1.1 (con't)	**Strand: Earth and Space Science** **Topic: Earth in the Solar System** **Grade Level 6-8**
How All Students Can Participate in this Activity Addressing Learning Standard(s):	**Possible Assessment Strategies and Portfolio Products**
As Written for This Grade Level Sonia and her lab group select 10 objects of different masses to test. They test the force of gravity on these objects by dropping them from their second-story classroom. For each object, they record the time it takes to fall to the ground and plot mass vs. time on a graph to assess their findings.	• Data chart showing Sonia's ability to determine force of gravity on objects • Videotape of Sonia's participation in this experiment with her lab partners • Hypothesis formulated by Sonia and her group • Lab report written by Sonia using scientific procedure • Graph of mass vs. time for the objects used in Sonia's lab group's experiment
At Lower Levels of Complexity (Entry Points) Milos uses a spring balance to weigh each object chosen by his lab group. After participating in the experiment with his peers, Milos records the data on a spreadsheet and generates a graph of the results.	• Data chart showing Milos's ability to weigh objects • Milos's chart recording the actual weight of each object • Videotape of Milos using the spring balance to weigh selected objects • Milos's self-generated graph of the weight of each object
Addressing Access Skills embedded in academic Instruction Lester helps select the objects for experimentation. He follows directions to drop and test each object with his lab group.	• Field data chart showing Lester's ability to drop/test each object within 5 seconds of a request • Line or bar graph summarizing the field data chart

Sometimes states create extensions for each of the Common Core State Standards. Here are some examples from the Colorado Department of Education. Used with permission.[6]

Table 1.2	**Reading Standards: Literature**
	Eighth Grade

Key Ideas and Details	Extension
Cite the textual evidence that most strongly supports an analysis of what the text says explicitly as well as inferences drawn from the text.	Answer simple literary questions based on a completed graphic organizer comparing characters or other story elements in a picture-based, 5-10 sentence passage.
Craft and Structure	**Extension**
Determine the meaning of words and phrases as they are used in a text, including figurative and connotative meanings; analyze the impact of specific word choices on meaning and tone, including analogies or allusions to other texts.	Identify the meaning of simple idiomatic phrases used in a story by matching with their concrete meanings.
Integration of Knowledge and Ideas	**Extension**
Analyze the extent to which a filmed or live production of a story or drama stays faithful to or departs from the text or script, evaluating the choices made by the director or actors.	Compare characters in written text read aloud with those in film version.
Range of Reading and Level of Text Complexity	**Extension**
By the end of the year, read and comprehend literature, including stories, dramas, and poems at the high end of grades 6–8 text complexity band independently and proficiently.	Participate in reading activities in adapted 8th grade literature.

Used with permission from The Colorado Department of Education http://www.cde.state.co.us/cdeassess/UAS/CoAcademicStandards.

Not all members of the IEP team may have seen these standards or curricular resources. One or more members of the team may want to share copies of key resources related to this student's grade level. The general education teacher who is a member of the IEP team also can serve as a resource person to the team in understanding the focus of the academic content for this grade level. In high school, it may be important to have general education teachers from each major content area provide input.

Camilla's Scenario

Camilla is a 12-year old 7th grader with severe disabilities. Her IEP team includes Camilla, her parents, the special education teacher, speech therapist, physical therapist, occupational therapist, and the general education teachers from the 7th grade team to which Camilla is assigned. Mr. Hargrove, a 7th grade teacher, gave Camilla's parents and therapists copies of the state standards and 7th grade learning goals prior to the IEP meeting. He also read them with Camilla prior to the meeting. At the meeting he had each 7th grade teacher describe curricular priorities for the year.

Guideline Two:
Become Familiar with the State's Approach to Extending Standards for AA-AAS

Camilla's state provides extensions for all the Common Core State Standards on the state website. The IEP team can refer to these in deciding how to access the grade level content standards.

As described earlier, states can use alternate achievement standards in considering Adequate Yearly Progress (AYP) for up to 1% of students with significant cognitive disabilities Many states provide curricular frameworks or extensions for the state standards for use in planning for students who take the AA-AAS. These extensions are not different content than the content standards. In fact, states must be careful that their AA-AAS align with content standards as one step in demonstrating the technical adequacy of this assessment system.

Camilla's Scenario, continued . . .

Camilla's state provides extension of all the Common Core State Standards in Mathematics and English Language Arts and has extensions for the state standards in science. Because Camilla is in the 7th grade, her teacher makes copies of the extensions for this grade level for reference at the IEP meeting. These extensions are a fairly long list in each content area. The teacher studies them carefully before the IEP team meeting. At the meeting, the Language Arts, Mathematics, and Science teachers are interested to see how the core standards have been extended for students who take the AA-AAS. Mrs. Beck, the special education teacher, explains to Camilla's parents how the extensions have been developed to help students like her access the state standards and are used by the state to develop the alternate assessment.

Guideline Three:
Keep the Planning Student-Focused

Sometimes the state standards and requirements for assessment may seem to overwhelm the IEP process. To keep the planning focused on this student's individual needs, begin with an overview of recent progress and strengths. The student might lead the meeting by reviewing recent achievements (e.g., with a Power Point presentation). Members of the team who have conducted recent assessments and worked with the student can present their findings to begin building a consensus of the student's educational needs. The student's preferences and individual goals can then provide a starting point for planning. The team should consider the student's current performance in academics, communication, and other areas to identify skills that can be used to promote access to the grade level content and accommodations and supports that will be needed.

Camilla's Scenario, continued . . .

Camilla is learning to direct her own IEP meetings. She begins the meeting by using her AAC device to give a greeting and to ask participants to introduce themselves. After the introductions, she presents a Power Point presentation of her recent achievements. Next, team members summarize her present level of performance. Camilla then continues her Power Point presentation showing pictures of her preferences and goals. Both Camilla's goals and the various team members' reports produce draft goals for the IEP that focus on Camilla's need to expand her communication skills, improve range of motion, and participate more in her personal care. She asks for goals related to her love of swimming, to have more time with friends, and to use the computer. Her parents affirm these goals and note their priority that the team "not give up" on teaching reading to Camilla.

Guideline Four:
Consider Both Specific Academic Goals and Broad Access Goals

With student individual needs and preferences articulated, the team can consider ways to access the grade level content that will be meaningful for this student and address the state's standards. At this point in the meeting it may be helpful for the general education teachers to discuss the highlights of the curriculum for that grade level, and for the team to have the state standards in front of them. In selecting goals, the team should consider each academic content area. The team should not try to recreate this entire curriculum on the IEP, for example, by writing a goal for every science unit. Instead, the team should focus on priorities for academic learning and skills to access the broader curriculum. The following figure illustrates how the IEP creates access to the curriculum. Note that the IEP is not meant to be a curriculum.

The IEP Creates Access to the Curriculum—

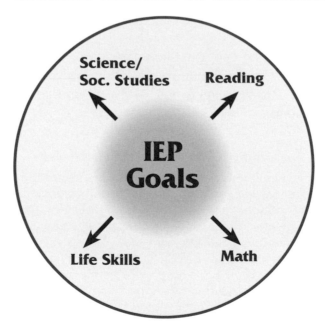

—but Is Not Itself a Curriculum

Camilla's Scenario, continued . . .

In reviewing both the science and math standards, the team realized that Camilla did not have the symbols in her AAC system to be able to communicate math and science concepts. They developed an IEP that focused on increasing her use and comprehension of 20 key words and symbols that she would frequently encounter in these subjects. For both social studies and science, Camilla would need an alternative to the paper and pencil activities that were frequently used by the class. The team determined that another access goal, one that would also relate to her preference for computers, would be to learn to select a picture from an array of pictures from her online textbook and related resources to express key concepts. One of the specific math skills for her to master this year, as the 7th graders focused on data compilation and analysis, was the preparation of graphs using spreadsheet software. They talked with Camilla about making some graphs related to her swimming activities. To participate more fully in 7th grade English Language Arts, the team targeted having Camilla select pictures to identify the main idea, conflict, and resolution from a narrative text read to her by one of her friends. To keep working towards reading, they also decided to have her participate in a remedial reading class that used systematic phonics instruction. They also decided to use short summaries of novels from English class or information from Social Studies written using a software program that generates picture-word symbols. The teacher would begin with single words and short phrases and build toward passage reading.

Guideline Five:
Ask the Question, "Is it Really Academic?"

After choosing some academic content and access skills, it is important for the team to take a second look at the goals and consider the question, "Is this really English Language Arts?" (or math, science, social studies). Sometimes in extending the state standard, the essence of the academic component is lost. The general education teachers can be especially helpful as resource people in making sure that the final goals have clear links to academic content. Consider the following examples to see how some align more closely to the original content.

In social studies and science, Camilla needs an alternative to the paper and pencil activities frequently used by the class. So the IEP team determined that an access goal related to her preference for computers would be learning to select one picture from an array of pictures from her online textbook and related resources to express key concepts.

The Common Core State Standard[7]

Content Area English Language Arts: Reading Standards for Literature (7th Grade)

Key Ideas and Details

Determine a theme or central idea of a text and analyze its development over the course of the text; provide an objective summary of the text.

Example 1

Camilla will use her AAC device to greet peers in English class.

Is this really English Language Arts?

No, although this is an important social skill the team will probably want to keep on the IEP, it is not an English Language Arts skill. Camilla needs additional English Language Arts objectives that focus on elements of literature.

No.

Example 2

Camilla will acquire 20 sight words that relate to activities in her community and home.

Is this really English Language Arts?

Yes, it's reading, but it does not link to the Common Core State Standard that other 7th graders will be learning. Again, the IEP team may keep this objective, but more work is needed to access the general curriculum.

Yes, but it doesn't align.

[7] http://www.corestandards.org/the-standards/english-language-arts-standards/reading-literature-6-12/grade-7/

Example 3

Camilla will select two major themes using pictures with phrases after hearing a text summary read aloud. She will categorize 2-3 events in each chapter of the text during read alouds using additional pictures related to the story, and will summarize by presenting a chart of these categories.

Is this really English Language Arts?

Yes. Notice that the **content** of the standard is the theme of the text. Camilla's objective focuses on identifying themes. The **performance** expected in the original standard is threefold: to determine, analyze, and summarize this theme. Note that the objective targets alternative ways for Camilla to perform all three of these strategies by using pictures and categorization. Although Camilla cannot read 7th grade passages, she can access age-appropriate literature by listening to text or summaries of text read to her by her teacher and peers. Given Camilla's grade level, these text summaries will likely be adapted from novels, as from other books, with a couple of paragraphs for each chapter. The teacher may focus on one chapter at a time. To help Camilla have an organizational framework for the novel, the teacher might use an overview of the text (e.g., the preview given on the back cover of the novel). From this, Camilla is taught to find the matching theme pictures. Then, as the teacher presents each chapter, Camilla creates an organizational framework categorizing events that occur in the chapter by these themes on two posters using pictures. By the end of the novel, her posters provide a tool to present a summary of the novel. She can then be taught to summarize the novel by communicating each theme and its sub event.

Yes, this is a well-aligned objective!

Example 4

Camilla will identify initial consonant and vowel sounds, and use this skill writing words with software that anticipates the spelling from the first letters.

Is this really English Language Arts?

Phonemic awareness is a critical step towards learning to read. This objective is important to Camilla as she learns the decoding skills to become an independent reader. However, this objective does **not** align with the 7th grade state standard, so something more is needed (e.g., see Example 3.) In contrast, it **will** be on her IEP as a target for promoting beginning reading.

Yes, this is a goal that broadly accesses the curriculum!

Guideline Six:
Do Not "Force Fit" All IEP Goals and Objectives into Alignment with Academic Standards

Students with moderate and severe disabilities may require therapy and life skills goals that will be part of the IEP but do not have any clear links to state standards. They may also need some remedial academic work like Camilla's ongoing acquisition of decoding skills for reading. A standards-based IEP for students with moderate and severe disabilities may have some goals that do not align with state standards. However, an IEP team can get off track if it begins with the therapy, remedial academic, and life skills goals and tries to back map them to grade level content standards. For example, a student may need to continue learning toileting skills. Trying to determine a language arts or math standard that links to toileting can either be a waste of time or promote instruction that infringes on personal privacy and dignity. Toileting is a legitimate goal in itself that need not link to an academic content standard. A better approach is to develop academic goals by beginning with the academic content standards rather than trying to back map functional goals into the grade-level standards.

Writing Measurable IEP Goals

All goals that are written should be measurable. A measurable goal, formulated clearly in writing, is one whose specific objectives the entire IEP team, or any one else working with the student, can agree have been met. The following are examples of non-measurable and measurable goals:

Non-Measurable Goal	Measurable Goal
Joyce will improve her comprehension. (Improve how?)	After participating in a read aloud of grade-appropriate text, Joyce will identify four elements of the narrative (character, setting, event, problem).
Nick will increase his graphing skills (Increase to what?)	When given access to computer graphing software, Nick will convert a table of numbers into three types of graphs.
Barry will identify the science concept. (What concept should he identify?)	After participating in an inquiry lesson and given a key vocabulary word, Barry will fill in a concept statement using this word—e.g., water that falls from clouds is called _____. (precipitation)

Writing Measurable IEP Objectives[8]

In developing the IEP, it is important to write objectives that have several qualities. First, short-term objectives should provide a progression towards achievement of the annual goal. Second, the objectives should target skills that are clearly measurable. These objectives should also target active student participation.

Developing Short-Term Objectives

Once the IEP team has identified general goals for the student, it's important to translate them into specific, measurable short-term objectives. To define these objectives, consider the student's present level of performance related to the annual goal. For example, one of Camilla's goals was to select pictures to represent concepts in her academic studies. Currently, Camilla can select some picture symbols on her AAC device. She also will point to pictures in a magazine when asked questions like, "Where is the dog?" In contrast, she has not yet learned to use pictures to represent broader concepts (e.g., map of the United States to represent that country). The team can build from this present level to an annual goal, by writing objectives that fill in the levels between the two points. Transforming Camilla's present level of performance to an annual goal may look like this:

	Camilla's Objectives
Present Level of Performance	Camilla uses pictures on her AAC device to ask for basic needs and to greet friends. She also will point to pictures of familiar objects or people. She does not yet use pictures to represent a concept.
Objective 1	Given 30 new pictures and symbols presented on the computer selected from the content areas, Camilla will select the picture or symbol named.
Objective 2	Given a three-choice array of pictures that relate to the lesson, and asked to show me ___ (e.g., "tornado"), Camilla will select the picture that shows the concept for 10 new concepts each quarter.
Objective 3	When asked, "What was the lesson about today?" Camilla will select a picture from a three-choice array.
Annual Goal	Given a variety of academic topics, Camilla will select pictures to represent major concepts described in class.

[8] This information on writing IEP objectives is adapted from Bateman and Herr, *Writing Measurable IEP Goals and Objectives*, Attainment Company/IEP Resources Publication (2003).

Writing Goals and Objectives for Active Participation

As the IEP team is developing measurable goals and objectives, it's important to consider how the student can be an active learner.

Active participation occurs in the general curriculum when the student acquires independent responses that demonstrate understanding of the academic content standard. In contrast, a "passive" skill is one in which the student simply has to cooperate with or tolerate physical or other guidance. For some students with severe intellectual and physical disabilities, it may be difficult to target an independent response, but active participation is possible if the student has at least one voluntary movement. For example, a student who has physical disabilities may not have the fine motor skills to point to a book that he would like read to him. A passive approach to this goal would be to use hand-over-hand assistance to help him choose a book. In this example, the teacher is actually making a choice for the student, leaving him with no independent response. The student's preference of book to be used for the literacy activity is not acknowledged. An active alternative would be to have the student use eye gaze (independent, voluntary response) to indicate which book he would like. Or, the student might use a switch connected to a computer that is scanning through book selections (independent, voluntary response). The following table provides several examples of how to modify objectives to promote active academic learning.

Table 2.1

Active Objectives for Academic Learning

Passive Responses (that don't require independent responses)	Active Responses (that simplify physical demands and focus on independence)
Brittany will circle the correct answer with physical guidance to answer comprehension questions.	Brittany will use a laser-head pointer (or small flashlight) to select between two pictures projected on a screen to answer comprehension questions (3 out of 5 correct).
Problem with this approach: *Brittany's physical disabilities do not permit her to use a pencil without help. This assistance can not be faded. There also is no way to determine if Brittany has any understanding of the task.*	**Advantage of this approach:** Brittany has the head control to move the light to her selection. Words can be presented with the pictures with the long-term goal of fading the use of pictures.
Kevin will listen to a story the teacher is reading.	Kevin will independently touch the page to indicate it is time to turn it after the teacher has read each page (with 75% accuracy).
Problem with this approach: *"Listening" is not an observable, measurable response. Students who are quiet and looking at the reader may not be attending. Kevin could be daydreaming.*	**Advantage of this approach:** Kevin is now actively engaged with the reader. Kevin might also have a goal like Brittany's to show comprehension. The teacher might also ask him to touch pictures on the page to answer questions about the story.
Kirsten will accompany her peer to buy lunch.	When at the cash register, Kirsten will ask a peer to help her purchase lunch by finding the symbol $ on her AAC device, to communicate "help me pay" (9 out of 10 trials).
Problem with this approach: *Kirsten is not performing any part of the academics of paying for her lunch; she is merely accompanying someone else.*	**Advantage of this approach:** Kirsten is now actively engaged in paying for her lunch. As she learns more about money she may indicate how much her peer should give the cashier.

Strategies for Alignment to State Standards

One of the most difficult challenges educators face is determining ways to make state standards accessible to students who currently have few academic skills. For example, how can a student with limited use of symbols access general curriculum that focuses on literary concepts in high school? Or, how can a student who is only beginning to recognize numbers access mathematics content that is introducing concepts like fractions? These are not easy questions to answer, but we would like to offer four ways to generate ideas for creating access to state standards. Each of these ideas will be described in the chapters to come.

• Select skills that promote overall English Language Arts and mathematics skills

• Focus on self-determination skills

• Using assistive technology to increase active, independent responding

• Use real-life activities to give meaning to the academic concept

Chapter 2

Presents the components of English Language Arts and mathematics, giving an explanation and examples of each component. Chapter 2 also includes ideas on how to consider different levels of symbols students may use.

Chapter 3

Describes how to focus components of self-determination. Ideas will be given about ways to incorporate self-determination skills into academic objectives.

Chapter 4

Explains how to create access to the general curriculum with the use of switches and augmentative and alternative communication devices. Chapter 4 will also give examples of software that may make access to the general curriculum possible. Examples of objectives that are made possible by the use of assistive technology will also be given.

Chapter 5

Reviews the concepts of real-life, age-appropriate activities. Chapter 5 will also review life skills domains and demonstrate how teachers can cross-reference academic components and real-life activities to create meaningful objectives.

Chapter 6

Provides a suggested practice routine for aligning objectives to the state standards by focusing on English Language Arts and mathematics skills, self-determination, assistive technology, and real-life activities. Chapter 6 also includes a case study.

Chapter 7

Gives an overview of effective instruction for teaching academic objectives to students with moderate and severe disabilities.

Chapter 2
Strategies for Alignment

Promote Broad Skills in English Language Arts and Mathematics

The first strategy to consider when creating IEP objectives that align with academic content standards is that of focusing on skills that promote broad concepts in English Language Arts (ELA) and mathematics. One of the challenges of developing standards-based IEPs is that the discrepancy between the student's assigned grade level (e.g., 8th grade) and instructional level (e.g., nonreader) may be large. But to address the student's current instructional level, the educational team selects specific objectives that promote student mastery of new ELA and mathematics skills while also teaching the concepts of grade-level content. Note that to promote mastery of these early ELA and mathematics skills concurrent with grade-level content, it's necessary to understand the components of these skills.

Promoting English Language Arts (ELA)

ELA Components

Many state standards in language arts parallel the Common Core State Standards in English Language Arts. The Common Core State Standards in English Language Arts include reading, writing, speaking and listening, and language. There also are ELA standards for history/social studies, science, and technology. Each strand (i.e., reading, writing, speaking and listening, and language) contains anchor standards that define expectations the students must meet to be prepared to enter college and workforce training programs. Table 2.1 explains the strands in English Language Arts and gives examples of standards that fall under each strand:

The Common Core State Standards in English Language Arts include reading, writing, speaking and listening, and language. There also are literacy standards for history/social studies, science, and technology.

Table 2.1

Common Core State Standards for English Language Arts
Strands and Examples of Standards[9]

Strands	Explanation	Examples of Standards			
READING: Standards for Literature		**Key Ideas and Details**	**Craft and Structure**	**Integration of Knowledge and Ideas**	**Range of Reading/ Level of Text Comprehension**
Text complexity and the growth of comprehension.	This strand emphasizes the increasing complexity of the text as well as the skill with which the student reads.	**Grade 5:** Determine a theme of a story, drama, or poem from details in the text, including how characters in a story or drama respond to challenges, or how the speaker in a poem reflects upon a topic; summarize the text.	**Grade 3:** Determine the meaning of words and phrases as they are used in a text, distinguishing literal from nonliteral language.	**Grade 9/10:** Analyze various accounts of a subject told in different mediums (e.g., a person's life story in both print and multimedia), determining which details are emphasized in each account.	**Grade 8:** Analyze the extent to which a filmed or live production of a story or drama stays faithful to or departs from the text or script, evaluating the choices made by the director or actors.
READING: Standards for Informational Text		**Key Ideas and Details**	**Craft and Structure**	**Integration of Knowledge and Ideas**	**Range of Reading/ Level of Text Comprehension**
Text details, structure, and meaning.	This strand emphasizes students reading text for detail, meaning, and comprehension.	**Grade 5:** Determine two or more main ideas of a text and explain how they are supported by key details; summarize the text.	**Grades 11/12:** Determine an author's point of view or purpose in a text in which the rhetoric is particularly effective, analyzing how style and content contribute to the power, persuasiveness, or beauty of the text.	**Grade 7:** Compare and contrast a text to an audio, video, or multimedia version of the text, analyzing each medium's portrayal of the subject (e.g., how the delivery of a speech affects the impact of the words).	**Grade 1:** With prompting and support, read informational texts appropriately complex for grade 1.

[9] http://www.corestandards.org/the-standards/english-language-arts-standards/introduction/how-to-read-the-standards/

Common Core State Standards for English Language Arts
Strands and Examples of Standards

Strands	Explanation	Examples of Standards			
READING: Standards Foundational Skills (Only K-5)		**Print Concepts**	**Phonological Awareness**	**Phonics and Word Recognition**	**Fluency**
Concepts of print, the alphabetic principle, and other basic conventions of the English writing system.	This strand emphasizes the development of readers that comprehend texts across a range of types and disciplines.	**Grade K:** Demonstrate understanding of the organization and basic features of print.	**Grade 1:** Demonstrate understanding of spoken words, syllables, and sounds (phonemes).	**Grade 3:** Decode multisyllable words.	**Grade 5:** Read with sufficient accuracy and fluency to support comprehension.
WRITING		**Texts and Type of Purpose**	**Production and Distribution of Writing**	**Research to Build and Present Knowledge**	**Range of Writing**
Text types, responding to reading, and research.	This strand focuses on writing skills (e.g., planning, revising, editing, etc.) as well as types of writing (i.e., arguments, informative/ explanatory texts, narratives). Research standards are also included in the writing strand.	**Grade 2:** Write opinion pieces in which they introduce the topic or book they are writing about, state an opinion, supply reasons that support the opinion, use linking words (e.g., because, and, also) to connect opinion and reasons, and provide a concluding statement or section.	**Grade 2:** With guidance and support from adults and peers, focus on a topic and strengthen writing as needed by revising and editing.	**Grade 3:** Recall information from experiences or gather information from print and digital sources; take brief notes on sources and sort evidence into provided categories.	**Grade 3:** Write routinely over extended time frames (time for research, reflection, and revision) and shorter time frames (a single sitting or a day or two) for a range of discipline-specific tasks, purposes, and audiences.
		Grade 7: Write arguments to support claims with clear reasons and relevant evidence.	**Grade 9/10:** Produce clear and coherent writing in which the development, organization, and style are appropriate to task, purpose, and audience.	**Grade 6:** Gather relevant information from multiple print and digital sources; assess the credibility of each source; and quote or paraphrase the data and conclusions of others while avoiding plagiarism and providing basic bibliographic information for sources.	**Grade 7:** Write routinely over extended time frames (time for research, reflection, and revision) and shorter time frames (a single sitting or a day or two) for a range of discipline-specific tasks, purposes, and audiences.

Common Core State Standards for English Language Arts
Strands and Examples of Standards

Strands	Explanation	Examples of Standards			
SPEAKING AND LISTENING		**Comprehension and Collaboration**		**Presentation of Knowledge and Ideas**	
Flexible communication and collaboration.	This strand includes skills needed to develop oral communication and interpersonal skills. Skills necessary for formal presentations are also part of this strand.	**Grade 7:** Delineate a speaker's argument and specific claims, evaluating the soundness of the reasoning and the relevance and sufficiency of the evidence.		**Grade 3:** Report on a topic or text, tell a story, or recount an experience with appropriate facts and relevant, descriptive details, speaking clearly at an understandable pace.	
LANGUAGE		**Conventions of Standard English**	**Knowledge of Language**	**Vocabulary Acquisition and Use**	
Conventions, effective use, and vocabulary.	This strand emphasizes rules of written and spoken English and includes standards that focus on vocabulary.	**Grade 1:** Spell untaught words phonetically, drawing on phonemic awareness and spelling conventions.	**Grade 11-12:** Interpret figures of speech (e.g., hyperbole, paradox) in context and analyze their role in the text.	**Grade 8:** Consult general and specialized reference materials (e.g., dictionaries, glossaries, thesauruses), both print and digital, to find the pronunciation of a word, or determine or clarify its precise meaning or its part of speech.	

Students with moderate and severe disabilities may continue to build foundational reading skills in later grades. For example, a 5th grade student may be beginning to read a 1st grade-level passage independently. When planning the IEP, It is important to target objectives that continue to promote independence in reading. If the student is past the level of the Foundational Skills standards, these may be considered remedial reading skills. The National Reading Panel identified five essential components of reading, including:

1. Phonemic awareness

2. Phonics

3. Fluency

4. Vocabulary

5. Text comprehension

Phonemic awareness is the ability to recognize the individual sounds, or phonemes, in spoken words. This skill is critically important so students can learn to associate phonemes in words and the letters that represent these sounds. Early phonemic awareness may involve word awareness. For example, the student may select a picture symbol to complete a repeated story line. The student may also begin to recognize if words rhyme. Next the student learns to recognize words that begin with the same sound and finally to pronounce the separate sounds in a word like "jam" /j/ /a/ /m/.

Phonics is the ability to pair spoken sounds and the letters in words. Phonics gives students the skills they need to decode and spell new words. Students pair knowledge of the printed alphabet with the phonemes in a word. While students may master learning to read some words "on sight," phonics is critical to learning to read.

Fluency is the skill to read text quickly and accurately. Fluency is associated with the comprehension of text. To understand the text, students need to be able to recognize most words at a single glance and read text smoothly and accurately.

Vocabulary is also important in learning to read. Students need to learn to recognize words quickly and comprehend what these words mean. Students with moderate and severe disabilities may learn to recognize large numbers of sight words, but have little use for this knowledge if they do not know what the words mean. Students need to learn the meaning of words that are not already part of their communication system.

Comprehension involves gaining meaning from both individual words and passages. Even before students learn to decode or recognize printed words, they begin to acquire comprehension skills through listening to passages that are read and to demonstrate understanding. They can also help to compose stories using their communication system.

Present Level of Performance

To consider how to promote early ELA skills while focusing on state standards, it is also important to consider present level of performance. One way to do this is to identify the extent to which the student currently uses symbols and displays the essential components of reading.

Beginning with Symbols/Pre-Literacy

Some students have not yet acquired the skills to discriminate between pictures or other symbols. They may have IEP objectives on learning to use an AAC system or other form of assistive technology. They may currently rely on nonsymbolic communication like sounds, movement and facial expressions. These students may also have few current literacy skills. They may not yet interact with books or listen to stories. One key point in working with students who are beginning with symbols is to be sure to use pictures, objects, and even text with all students. Once students master the assistive technology offered, they may make rapid progress in demonstrating understanding. To withhold symbols until students are somehow "ready" may place a ceiling on performance. At the very least, it does no harm to make symbols available to students. For this level of student, the highest priority is to learn use of an AAC system and begin to understand as well as produce symbols.

Some of the skills that might be taught to access English Language Arts for students who are beginning with symbols are as follows. Jordan is a student who will be learning to use AAC concurrently with his reading lessons in 3rd grade:

Jordan's Examples

When given familiar sentences, Jordan will select an object/picture to complete the sentences (4 of 5 correct).

Jordan will use eye gaze to choose a book he would like read to him.

Jordan will indicate when to turn the page by hitting a switch when the reader pauses.

After a story has been read to him, Jordan will correctly select an object/picture that identifies the main idea of the story.

"Be sure to introduce symbols like pictures, objects, and text with all students so as not to place a ceiling on their performance."

Early Symbolic Use and Emerging Literacy/English Language Arts

Students at this second level are beginning to use some symbols including objects, pictures or a few sight words.

For example, the student may use a picture schedule to complete daily activities. Or the student may be able to find her name on a wall chart. The student may also have some emergent literacy skills like turning the pages of a book or pointing to the book title. Students at this level will be learning to apply these skills to broader reading activities, as shown in these examples for Chondra, a 7th grader:

Chondra's Examples

Chondra will prepare Power Point presentations using pictures for the main ideas.

Chondra will identify the main characters of a story by using pictures/initial letter sounds for their names. (Using summaries of 7th grade books shortened and adapted for simplified vocabulary.)

Chondra will use IntelliKeys to compose sentences by selecting and sequencing key sight words.

Symbolic Language Arts

Students at the third level have mastered some sight words, and may have some functional academic skills locating community signs like restrooms. Research on who takes AA-AAS indicates that most students in "the 1%" have some symbol use.[10] These students are ready to begin expanding their use of symbols to build language arts skills. They may have had extensive instruction in functional reading to learn everyday sight words, but have not learned how to apply skills in an age-appropriate academic curriculum. The following examples are for Linda, a 10 year-old student who has a 50-sight-word vocabulary and can use words to perform daily living activities like preparing simple recipes. She will look at magazines and find sight words in a Word Find Puzzle. She is just beginning to receive instruction in the 5th grade reading program. Her objectives might include:

Linda's Examples

Linda will spell 20 familiar sight words and 10 novel words (to learn letter-sound associations).

Linda will apply her emerging spelling skills to compose brief notes/email messages using word prediction software (that offers several word choices as each letter is entered).

Linda will apply her word finding skills to locate character names and key facts to comprehend a passage.

Addressing Both Grade-Level Standards and Present Level of Performance

Once grade-level standards and present level of ELA skills are known, educators can plan ways to address both the grade-level standards and present level of ELA performance. As explained in Chapter 1, it's important for you to focus on aligning to the students' assigned grade-level standards. With creativity, your team may also find ways to promote emerging literacy while addressing these standards. So instead of beginning at some lower grade level (e.g., Kindergarten standards) and trying to work up to student age levels (e.g., 8th grade), your team should begin with the age level (8th grade) and incorporate objectives that will promote ELA skills from the student's present level of performance. Table 2.2 gives examples of ELA skills that address state standards at different symbolic levels to show how to blend the concepts of grade level alignment and present level of performance.

[10] Towles-Reeves, E., Kleinert, H., & Muhomba, M. (2009). Alternate assessment: Have we learned anything now? Exceptional Children, 75, 233-252.

Table 2.2	Examples of Aligning to the Grade-Level Standard that Incorporate Student's Present Level of Performance (Using the Common Core State Standards)[11]	
Strand: Category of standard	**Grade-level standard**	**Objectives based on different present levels of performance**
Language **Conventions of Standard English**	**2nd Grade** Demonstrate command of the conventions of standard English capitalization, punctuation, and spelling when writing: Consult reference materials, including beginning dictionaries, as needed to check and correct spellings.	Ricky will select capital letter and correct spelling for his name and then add a period to the end of sentences on each page for 4 out of 5 worksheets. Nick will use software prompts (e.g., color coding of misspelled word) to locate where capitalization or punctuation or change in spelling are needed in creating correct word/picture sentences with at least 5 out of 7 correct. Jackie will proofread her writing by using spell check software to confirm spelling and software prompts to add capitalization and punctuation with no more than 1 error remaining per page.
Reading: Literature **Integration of Knowledge and Ideas**	**4th Grade** Compare and contrast the treatment of similar themes and topics (e.g., opposition of good and evil) and patterns of events (e.g., the quest) in stories, myths, and traditional literature from different cultures.	Leslie will select object/pictures to compare two multicultural story themes for 4 out of 5 opportunities. Adam will use pictures to identify themes in multicultural literature read to him and sort the different stories by corresponding themes for 4 out of 5 opportunities. Thomas will use a Venn diagram to compare and contrast the themes of multicultural literature he has previously read with 90% responses correct for at least 3 stories.

[11] http://www.corestandards.org/the-standards/english-language-arts-standards

Examples of Aligning to the Grade-Level Standard that Incorporate Student's Present Level of Performance
(Using the Common Core State Standards)

Strand: Category of standard	Grade level standard	Objectives based on different present levels of performance
Speaking and Listening **Comprehension and Collaboration**	**8th Grade** Engage effectively in a range of collaborative discussions (one-on-one, in groups, and teacher-led) with diverse partners on grade 8 topics, texts, and issues, building on others' ideas and expressing their own clearly.	Lisa will develop a log of her favorite stories by selecting icons/book jackets on the computer and share this log to build on the ideas of a book group for 2 out of 3 opportunities. John will indicate his agreement/disagreement with 9 of 10 viewpoints offered by others in a discussion group and use pictures/phrases to indicate why for each during 2 out of 3 discussions. Kerri will lead a small group in a book discussion by reading a list of 5 questions she generates in advance and then contribute to the discussion by indicating "I agree/disagree because . . ." for 2 out of 3 opportunities.
Writing **Production and Distribution of Writing**	**9th-10th Grade** Use technology, including the Internet, to produce, publish, and update individual or shared writing products, taking advantage of technology's capacity to link to other information and to display information flexibly and dynamically.	George will contribute to a group multimedia presentation by selecting 5 images from the Internet. Melissa will select material from internet sites using the copy/paste functions to create a Power Point presentation on a selected topic that includes at least 5 related slides. Jerry will find websites that link to the topic of a shared writing product and will correctly link the websites to the product using hyperlinks for 4 out of 5 opportunities.

Examples of Aligning to the Grade-Level Standard that Incorporate Student's Present Level of Performance
(Using the Common Core State Standards)

Strand: Category of standard	Grade level standard	Objectives based on different present levels of performance
Reading: Foundational Skills **Fluency**	**3rd Grade:** Read with sufficient accuracy and fluency to support comprehension: Read grade-level prose and poetry orally with accuracy, appropriate rate, and expression.	Helen will pace a story read by a peer by turning each of 10 pages within 10 seconds of when the peer stops reading the page. Brad will listen to a book on CD using picture cues/ sight words to keep pace with the CD for at least 10 pages. Stephanie will read story summaries of 3rd grade stories that incorporate her current sight word/ decoding skills at a rate of 20 words/ minute with 90% accuracy.
English/Language Arts **History/Social Studies** **Craft and Structure**	**11th-12th Grade:** Evaluate authors' differing points of view on the same historical event or issue by assessing the authors' claims, reasoning, and evidence.	After participating in read-alouds of historical events by two authors with differing views, Craig will select pictures/objects to restate evidence/ claims each author stated for at least 3 pairs of passages. After participating in read-alouds of historical events by two authors with differing views, Keyona will use pictures to determine if the authors were pro/con and then select pictures/objects to indicate authors' reason for at least 3 different events. After reading brief summaries, Justin will use a graphic organizer to categorize 3 different authors' point of view on the same historical event as positive, negative, or neutral and will select one fact to support each choice and generalizes this skill across 4 different events.

Promoting Mathematics Skills

Components of Mathematics

Similar to ELA, teachers can also create access to mathematics grade-level standards while promoting basic concepts of mathematics. Many states developed their mathematics standards to be consistent with those proposed by the Common Core State Standards. The CCSS in Mathematics are divided into two types of Standards: the Standards for Mathematical Practice and the Standards for Mathematical Content. The Standards for Mathematical Process were derived from the process standards written by the National Council for Teachers of Mathematics (NCTM), and from the strands of mathematical proficiency written by the National Research Council. The standards describe "processes and proficiencies" that math educators should seek to develop in their students. The Standards for Mathematical Practices include the following: (a) make sense of problems and persevere in solving them; (b) reason abstractly and quantitatively; (c) construct viable arguments and critique the reasoning of others; (d) model with mathematics; (e) use appropriate tools strategically; (f) attend to precision; (g) look for and make use of structure; and (h) look for and express regularity in repeated reasoning.[12]

The Standards for Mathematical Content are divided by different domains and grade levels in K-8. The high school content standards are simply divided into domains. While it's important to locate the math standards for your specific state, the following tables illustrate the content standards of math likely to be addressed:

---

[12] http://www.corestandards.org/the-standards/mathematics/introduction/standards-for-mathematical-practice/

Table 2.3

Common Core State Standards
Mathematics
Domains and Examples of Standards in Grades K-8[13]

Domain/Grade Level	Overview of Domain	Examples of Standards
Counting and Cardinality **Kindergarten**	Represent whole numbers with sets of objects, write numbers, count sequence to 100; compare numbers.	**Kindergarten** When counting objects, say the number names in the standard order, pairing each object with one, and only one, number name; and each number name with one, and only one, object.
Operations and Algebraic Thinking **Grades K-5**	Represent and solve problems involving addition, subtraction, multiplication and division; understand the properties of the operations; generate and analyze patterns and relationships.	**Grade 3:** Fluently multiply and divide within 100, using strategies such as the relationship between multiplication and division (e.g., knowing that $8 \times 5 = 40$, or that $40 \div 5 = 8$) or properties of operations. By the end of Grade 3, know from memory all products of two one-digit numbers.
Numbers and Operations in Base Ten **Grades K-5**	Understand the place value system; use this system and properties of operations to solve problems.	**Grade 5:** Use place value understanding to round decimals to any place.
Numbers and Operations-Fractions **Grades 3-5**	Understand fractions as numbers; use equivalent factions to add and subtract.	**Grade 4:** Understand addition and subtraction of fractions as joining and separating parts referring to the same whole.
Measurement and Data **Grades K-5**	Measure and estimate length, weight, and capacity directly and indirectly; work with time and money; represent and interpret data.	**Grade 2:** Measure the length of an object twice, using length units of different lengths for the two measurements; describe how the two measurements relate to the size of the unit chosen.
Geometry **Grades K-8**	Identify, name and describe shapes using their properties; analyze, compare, create, compose, and reason with shapes; graph points on a plane; solve real-world problems involving area, perimeter, volume, surface area, and angle measure; understand and apply the Pythagorean Theorem.	**Grade 6:** Represent three-dimensional figures using nets made up of rectangles and triangles, and use the nets to find the surface area of these figures. Apply these techniques in the context of solving real-world and mathematical problems.

[13] http://www.corestandards.org/the-standards/mathematics

Common Core State Standards Mathematics
Domains and Examples of Standards in Grades K-8

Domain/Grade Level	Overview of Domain	Examples of Standards
Ratios and Proportional Relationships **Grades 6-7**	Understand and use ratios to solve problems; analyze and use proportional relationships to solve problems.	**Grade 7:** Identify the constant of proportionality (unit rate) in tables, graphs, equations, diagrams, and verbal descriptions of proportional relationships.
The Number System **Grades 6-8**	Find common factors and multiples; work with rational and irrational numbers.	**Grade 8:** Know that numbers that are not rational are called irrational. Understand informally that every number has a decimal expansion; for rational numbers show that the decimal expansion repeats eventually, and convert a decimal expansion which repeats eventually into a rational number.
Expressions and Equations **Grades 6-8**	Solve one variable equations and inequalities; analyze and solve linear equations; generate equivalent expressions; work with radicals and integer exponents.	**Grade 6:** Write and evaluate numerical expressions involving whole-number exponents.
Statistics and Probability **Grades 6-8**	Summarize and describe distribution; draw inferences about populations; investigate patterns of association; develop, use, and evaluate probability models.	**Grade 7:** Use data from a random sample to draw inferences about a population with an unknown characteristic of interest. Generate multiple samples (or simulated samples) of the same size to gauge the variation in estimates or predictions.
Functions **Grade 8**	Define, evaluate, and compare functions; use functions to model relationships and quantities.	**Grade 8:** Understand that a function is a rule that assigns to each input exactly one output. The graph of a function is the set of ordered pairs consisting of an input and the corresponding output.

Table 2.4

Common Core State Standards
Mathematics-High School
Domains and Examples of Standards in High School[14]

Domain	Overview of Domain	Examples of Standards
Numbers and Quantity	Use properties of rational and irrational, and real and complex numbers; reason quantitatively and use units to solve problems; perform operations on matrices.	**The Real Number System** Explain why the sum or product of two rational numbers is rational; that the sum of a rational number and an irrational number is irrational; and that the product of a nonzero rational number and an irrational number is irrational. **Quantities** Define appropriate quantities for the purpose of descriptive modeling.
Algebra	Create, interpret and use polynomial expressions to represent and solve problems both graphically and symbolically.	**Seeing Structure in Expression** Interpret parts of an expression, such as terms, factors, and coefficients. **Creating Equations** Create equations in two or more variables to represent relationships between quantities; graph equations on coordinate axes with labels and scales.
Functions	Understand, interpret, and analyze linear, non-linear and trigonometric functions; use these functions to model and solve problems.	**Interpreting Functions** Use function notation, evaluate functions for inputs in their domains, and interpret statements that use function notation in terms of a context. **Trigonometric Functions** Prove the addition and subtraction formulas for sine, cosine, and tangent and use them to solve problems.

[14] http://www.corestandards.org/the-standards/mathematics

Table 2.4 (con't)	Common Core State Standards Mathematics-High School Domains and Examples of Standards in High School		
Domain	**Overview of Domain**	**Examples of Standards**	
Modeling	Understand the process and tools of modeling to understand and analyze a variety of situations.	According to the CCSS, "Modeling is best interpreted not as a collection of isolated topics but rather in relation to other standards. Making mathematical models is a Standard for Mathematical Practice, and specific modeling standards appear throughout the high school standards."[15]	
Geometry	Understand the concepts of congruence, similarity, and symmetry from analytic, symbolic, and coordinate systems perspectives under reflective, translational, and rotational transformations.	**Geometric Measurement and Dimension** Use volume formulas for cylinders, pyramids, cones, and spheres to solve problems. **Modeling with Geometry** Use geometric shapes, their measures, and their properties to describe objects (e.g., modeling a tree trunk or a human torso as a cylinder).	
Statistics & Probability	Use statistics to describe variability in data and to make informed decisions.	**Interpreting Categorical and Quantitative Data** Represent data with plots on the real number line (dot plots, histograms, and box plots). **Using Probability to Make Decisions** Calculate the expected value of a random variable; interpret it as the mean of the probability distribution.	

[15] http://www.corestandards.org/the-standards/mathematics/high-school-modeling/introduction/

Across the grade levels, students will address increasingly complex material on these components. For example, in the early grades students learn to recognize numbers and count. By the later grades, students are using more advanced concepts like fractions, exponents, and decimals. Similarly, in the early grades students may learn about basic measurements like weight and length. By later grades, they are learning about volume, area, and velocity.

Present Level of Performance in Mathematics

Similar to language arts, students' present level of performance in mathematics may be summarized based on their use of symbols and general knowledge of math. Students who have begun to use mathematic symbols like numerals and computation signs are able to respond in ways that can be used to access grade-level content more easily. Similarly, students who have some understanding of the everyday references to math concepts (e.g., which has "more") have a foundation for ongoing instruction. The following describe present level of performance in mathematics.

Beginning Symbolic and Few/No References to Math Concepts/Problems

For some students, the educational team will be planning access to grade-level math instruction without the benefit of the student having related symbolic communication. The beginning point for instruction will be to introduce symbols and concepts concurrent with exposure to the grade-level math content. For example, the student might learn the concept of numbers through "countdowns" related to daily routines (e.g., "Lift your arm to help me remove your coat when I count to three.") The student may begin learning concepts of "more" and "less than" (e.g., "Look up to indicate *more music*.") However, it is important that as the student is learning these concepts in activities outside of math, grade-level math content is also being modified for the student to participate in actively.

Early Symbolic and Emerging Math Concepts

Some students have learned to recognize numbers and to understand some everyday math concepts. But they may not yet know how to use these skills in the context of math instruction. For example, the student may have learned to point to numbers on a calendar, but not yet understand that a "5" relates to 5 items. The student may use a symbol to request "more" snack or time with a leisure material (by itself, not a math skill), but not realize that the concept can also be used to compare sets or sizes of items (a math skill). The student may use some counting (e.g., "get 4 cups to set the table") but not realize how to count on for addition (1, 2 cups and 3, 4). Or, the student may not comprehend the symbols for the task ($2 + 2 = 4$). These students will need specific instruction in beginning to use math symbols and concepts in the variety of activities presented for their assigned grade level.

Symbolic and Life Skills Math Concepts

Some students have made excellent progress in beginning math instruction and are able to tell time, count money, and use basic measurement for length and weight. They may be able to determine which of two prices is "less than," or count up from a price to determine the number of dollars needed to pay. However, some students also have gaps in their knowledge of math. They may have little understanding of geometry and become confused when asked to use concepts like shape, area, and perimeter in a job context. They may lack data analysis skills and not understand news polls and nutrition charts. These students will need additional instruction to use their math skills for more advanced math achievement.

Addressing Both Grade-Level Standards and Present Level of Performance for Mathematics

As with language arts, it's possible to address students' present level of performance while also considering their assigned grade-level in mathematics. In doing so, the educational team considers the essence of the grade-level standard along with ways to promote the students' mastery of mathematics. Table 2.5 illustrates this approach.

Table 2.5	Examples of Aligning to the Grade-Level Standard that Incorporate Student's Present Level of Performance (Standards from the Common Core State Standards)[16]	
Domain	**Grade-level standard**	**Objectives based on different present levels of performance**
Numbers and Operations- Fractions: **Developing understanding of fractions as numbers**	**3rd Grade:** Understand a fraction 1/b as the quantity formed by 1 part when a whole is partitioned into b equal parts; understand a fraction a/b as the quantity formed by a parts of size 1/b.	Ricky will match fractional numbers to a picture prior to taking that many pieces/ slices of a snack (e.g., "1" in ¼) for 3 fractions (¼, $^1/_3$, $^2/_3$). Nick will select the correct amount of a snack item when shown a diagram and told the fraction for 5 fractions (e.g., ¼, ½, $^2/_3$, $^1/_6$, $^3/_5$). Using a set model, Jackie will write a fraction to show how many items of a set are still available for use (e.g., = ● ● ○ 2 of 3 CDs are free).
Expressions and Equations: **Analyze and solve linear equations and pairs of simultaneous linear equations**	**7th Grade:** Give examples of linear equations in one variable with one solution, infinitely many solutions, or no solutions. Show which of these possibilities is the case by successively transforming the given equation into simpler forms, until an equivalent equation of the form $x = a$, $a = a$, or $a = b$ results (where a and b are different numbers).	Leslie will use the equal sign on her AAC device to indicate "same" or for 4 of 5 equations augmented with objects (e.g., ***= 3). Hannah will use a pictorial number line (e.g., numerals and correct number of dots) to solve linear equations with sums under 10 for 4 of 5 equations. Thomas will write the linear equation for 3 of 4 known money facts (e.g., x quarters = $1.00 or x (25) = 100).

[16] http://www.corestandards.org/the-standards/mathematics

Examples of Aligning to the Grade-Level Standard that Incorporate Student's Present Level of Performance
(Standards from the Common Core State Standards)

Domain	Grade-level standard	Objectives based on different present levels of performance
Geometry: **Draw and identify lines and angles, and classify shapes by properties of their lines and angles**	**4th Grade:** Draw points, lines, line segments, rays, angles (right, acute, obtuse), and perpendicular and parallel lines. Identify these in two-dimensional figures.	Jason will use objects or virtual manipulatives[17] to indicate the line between two points and to create rays of an angle for 2 of 3 hands on projects. John will use maps of familiar locations and find roads that form lines, line segments, angles, parallel, and perpendicular for 4 of 5 maps. Kerri will follow picture/word directions for a project in which she uses line segments, angles, perpendicular, and parallel lines (e.g., to build a flower box) and will label each on the finished product with 4 of 5 labels correct.
Measurement and Data: **Work with time and money**	**2nd Grade:** Tell and write time from analog and digital clocks to the nearest five minutes, using a.m. and p.m.	George (visually impaired) will push the button on a talking clock when asked, "What time is it?" for 4 of 5 trials. Melissa will match numbers on clocks to find the next activity on her schedule for 4 of 5 activities. Jerry will read numbers to 60 to tell time to the minute with a digital watch.

[17] Find virtual manipulatives at http://nlvm.usu.edu/en/nav/vlibrary.html

Examples of Aligning to the Grade-Level Standard that Incorporate Student's Present Level of Performance
(Standards from the Common Core State Standards)

Domain	Grade-level standard	Objectives based on different present levels of performance
Statistics and Probability: **Interpreting Categorical and Quantitative Data**	**High School** Represent data with plots on the real number line (dot plots, histograms, and box plots).	Helen will use an elimination graph (objects velcroed to graph) to indicate completion for 5 of 5 activities. Brad will label a histogram to display continuous scale data in intervals (e.g., days of the month with temperatures between 60-64, 65-69, 70-74, etc.) for 3 of 4 sets of data. Stephanie will generate a dot plot to display data she has collected (e.g., votes for senior class song) and interpret her data by correctly answering 4 of 5 related questions.

Chapter 3
Strategies for Alignment

Focus on Self-Determination

A second way to select objectives that align to academic standards for students with moderate and severe disabilities is to focus on instructing components of self-determination. Teaching self-determination skills to students with disabilities promotes their learning of skill sets that increase their chances of taking control of their lives in and out of school. One way to make grade-level standards meaningful for students with moderate and severe disabilities is to use general curriculum activities as context for learning self-determination skills that contribute to increased autonomy for students. These skills can promote learning of the general curriculum, while at the same time foster the acquisition of skills with lifelong benefits. To develop a focus on this area, the educational team should begin by reviewing the components of self-determination.

Components of Self-Determination

To achieve self-determination, students need to acquire the skills to direct their own lives and have the opportunity to learn, practice, and apply them in school, at home, and in other environments. Consider how general education teachers offer varied opportunities for students to direct their own learning. For example, their students may select the topic for a project, determine what activity to do first, negotiate an activity with peers, or develop a solution to a problem in a cooperative learning group. Similarly, students with moderate and severe disabilities need the same opportunity to be active in directing their learning. Examples of components of self-determination include the following:

One way to make grade level standards meaningful for students with moderate and severe disabilities is to use general curriculum activities as context for learning self-determination skills that contribute to increased autonomy for students.

Self-Determination Skills

Component	Example
Choice-Making	• Make choices within an activity • Choose between two or more activities
Decision-Making	• Decide topic for class project • Determine best resource to use to get information
Problem-Solving	• Look at a picture to determine why DVD player is not working • Identify three alternative ways character in story could resolve a conflict
Goal-Setting	• Set a goal for number of books to be read in a month • Identify and communicate IEP goals
Self-Management/Self-Evaluation	• Use a bar graph to track number of assignments completed • Rate self on how well performed on given assignment
Self-Awareness	• Develop picture/word list of likes and dislikes • Develop and learn to read a list of "facts about me"

Incorporating Self-Determination into Academic Objectives

As the IEP team considers the grade-level standard, its members may want to review each of the components of self-determination to determine how these skills might create access to this standard. In the following example, basic self-determination skills are incorporated with state standards in the social studies curriculum:

5th Grade Social Studies Standard

Compare and contrast the roles various religious and ethnic groups have played in the development of the United States with those of Canada, Mexico, and selected countries of Central America.

Walter's Scenario

Walter is 10 year old boy who is nonverbal and has autism. He can read about 10 sight words and count to 20. Walter's 5th grade social studies teacher likes to use both self-directed and cooperative learning activities. While both types of instruction provide the opportunity for Walter to develop age appropriate social skills that he currently lacks, his tendency to spend time alone engaged with his favorite objects and toys have made it difficult to get him participating in this class. The educational team considers ways to get Walter involved in social studies by focusing on self-determination. They decide to consider several components of self-determination to access this standard on ethnic diversity.

Choice

Walter currently will choose between food and leisure items. He has a strong interest in objects that provide auditory stimulation and will frequently make items drum, ping, or create other repetitive sounds.

They decide that one way Walter might begin to understand ethnic diversity is through the sounds of the everyday items and musical instruments distinctive to selected ethnic groups. These sounds will be associated with pictures of the ethnic group to which they belong.

> The IEP team decides that one way Walter might begin to understand ethnic diversity is through studying the sounds of the everyday items and musical instruments distinctive to these groups.

His objective might read something like this:

> Walter will choose items associated with various North American ethnic groups and then request the object using pictures of the group for 4 of 5 ethnic groups.

Self-Awareness

Walter's class will be doing projects in which they trace their ethnic and religious heritage for at least three generations. Walter comes from a family who immigrated to the U.S. from Poland in the 1940s. His family continues to have strong cultural ties to Polish food and to their Jewish heritage.

His parents note that Walter has some distinct food favorites and is participating in religious education. The team considers how Walter might create his own heritage report. They decide that each week Walter will receive instruction in using Power Point and selecting and inserting digital pictures, so that he will be able to independently select the final 10 pictures for his class presentation in the spring. His parents agree to contribute a large set of digital pictures for this project. Another objective for Walter might read something like this:

> Walter will select at least 10 digital pictures and sight word labels to create a power point presentation about his heritage.

Goal Setting

It's decided to teach Walter how to set a goal for the number of turns he will take in the cooperative learning activity. Staff will prompt his peers to give him easily understandable turns (e.g., to select the next picture, to help turn in their project, to pass items to a peer).

As part of the support Walter receives for his autism diagnosis, he is accustomed to a work system in which the teacher designates the number of responses expected in each lesson before a break. The teacher uses clips on a laminated chart for each item to be completed. As Walter completes each response, he removes a clip. He knows that when all the clips are removed, he can have a break with one of his preferred leisure items. The IEP team decides to teach Walter to set a goal for the number of turns he will take in the cooperative learning activity. The teachers will prompt his peers to give him easily understandable turns (e.g., to select the next picture, to turn in the project, to pass items to a peer). While not directly related to the standard on ethnic diversity, this participation will keep Walter actively engaged in each day's activities. The objective is the following:

> Walter will select clips to set a goal for the number of turns he will take in his cooperative learning group for 4 out of 5 days.

Expanding Academic Objectives to Include Self-Determination

In the last examples, ideas were provided for accessing an academic standard using self-determination skills.

Sometimes the team has targeted academic objectives, but they also want to use this learning as an opportunity to promote self-determination. The following are examples of academic objectives that were expanded to include functional skills helpful to attain self-determination:

Goal 1	**Eric's Example** Eric will count between 1 and 20 items with 9 out of 10 trials correct.
Goal 1 with Self-Determination Focus	Eric will choose a number and count items to represent that number. Eric will count tasks to determine how many jobs he completed.
Goal 2	**Stephanie's Example** Stephanie will select pictures to identify 2/3 of a story's main characters.
Goal 2 with Self-Determination Focus	Stephanie will select pictures to identify 2/3 of a story's main characters and choose one that is most like her in some way (self-awareness).

Goal 3	**Roxanne's Example** Roxanne will increase her sight word vocabulary to 50 words.
Goal 3 with Self-Determination Focus	Roxanne will increase her sight word vocabulary to 50 words including words that she can use to evaluate her daily work (e.g., "excellent," "okay," "not my best").
Goal 4	**Sam's Example** Sam will develop a picture/word journal.
Goal 4 with Self-Determination Focus	Sam will use a picture/word journal to rate characteristics of potential jobs based on likes/dislikes (self awareness, decision-making about future job).

Chapter 4
Strategies for Alignment

Using Assistive Technology

There are many forms of assistive technology. Low-tech assistive technology includes picture symbols, photographs, pencil grips, and stencils. Using any of these items, teachers can make academic standards more accessible to students. For example, students who are unable to read words may rely on picture symbols or photographs to gain meaning from text. Students who need assistance with the fine motor skills of writing may use pencil grips or stencils.

High-tech assistive technology includes computer programs, switches, and other devices. This type of assistive technology can be beneficial for students with physical disabilities and those with intellectual disabilities. For example, a Big Mack may be programmed to say a phrase for a student who cannot speak. Adapted keyboards may be used for students who do not have the physical ability to touch small keys.

Using switches and augmentative communication devices, students should able to engage in academics more independently. The following are examples of how students can access language arts and mathematics using high-tech assistive technology.

Reading

Attainment's
GoTalk 4+

Randy's Scenario

Every morning, Mrs. Jones reads a story to the class and then the class reads the story back to her, each student reading a separate sentence. Randy cannot read and is nonverbal, but his teacher would like him to participate in the class story reading activity. In order to help him participate, she programs his sentences into a **GoTalk 4+**, which contains four spaces for pictures. When it is Randy's turn to read, he touches the pictures on his GoTalk and "reads" his sentences to the class.

Kim's Scenario

RJ's MP3
Player-Drive

Kim is a 10th grader who has very limited movement. She is included in a language arts class. Each day in class the students are given time to read a chapter of the novel they are studying. Kim's teacher would like her to be able to read the chapters independently. Students in Kim's class have recorded a low vocabulary version of the novel as an MP3 file. Kim's teacher has attached a switch to **RJ's MP3 Player-Drive** in order for Kim to access the MP3 player. Kim is able to independently listen to the chapters through headphones. She puts on the headphones, then touches the switch which activates the MP3 player.

Writing

Matthew's Scenario

Attainment's
Touch Screen

Matthew is learning how to spell his name using word processing software. However, Matthew is unable to manipulate the mouse. Matthew's teacher has installed a touch screen on the computer. He is now able to touch the letters of his name on the screen as well as touch the print icon to print out his spelling assignment.

Jamie's Scenario

Jamie's class is creating a journal about their community-based experiences. Jamie is unable to write and cannot type. Her teacher has an **IntelliKeys** keyboard attached to the computer. With this keyboard, Jamie can touch large picture symbols that will help her write sentences. When she is finished creating the sentences, she can touch the print symbol to print out her sentences to be placed in her journal.

IntelliKeys Keyboard with overlay inserted

Math

Ryan's Scenario

Ryan likes to turn on appliances and toys using a switch and **Power Link**. However, he often turns things on at inappropriate times. Ryan's teacher would like him to begin understanding number concepts. Ryan's teacher now counts to a certain number before Ryan turns an object on. For example, during snack time, Ryan is going to activate a blender to make a milkshake. Ryan has now learned to wait until the count of 3, instead of activating the blender before his teacher is ready.

Power Link

Jennie's Scenario

Jennie needs to drink an 8 oz. protein shake for lunch each day. Her teacher would like her to learn to measure out the shake herself. However, it is hard for Jennie to hold the container. Jennie's teacher has hooked a switch to an automatic pourer. Jennie touches the switch and the pourer turns and begins to pour the shake into a measuring cup. When the liquid gets to 8 oz., Jennie touches the switch again and it stops pouring.

Automatic Pourer

Aside from switches and augmentative communication devices, there is also software that can make access to the general curriculum possible. On the following pages a number of software programs are listed with short explanations to highlight which skills are addressed by each program.

Reading

Software	Skills/Concepts Taught
Bailey's Book House (www.attainmentcompany.com)	Through interactive software and a supplemental workbook, students can learn about words, rhyming, prepositions, adjectives, and sentence building.
Nouns and Sounds (www.laureatelearning.com)	A program that trains discrimination of environmental sounds and encourages individuals to match these sounds with realistic photographs; builds auditory awareness and listening skills.
News-2-You (http://news2you.n2y.com)	A weekly current events newspaper illustrated with simple line drawings.
Simon Sounds It Out http://www.donjohnston.com/products/simon_sio/	An animated personal tutor helps students with letter sounds, word families, onsets, and rhymes.
Early Literacy Skills Builder (www.attainmentcompany.com)	A *research-based*, language-rich literacy curriculum for children ages 5 to 10 with moderate to severe developmental disabilities. It incorporates systematic instruction to teach both print and phonemic awareness.
Picture It (www.slatersoftware.com)	Can be used to support creative writing for students or adapt classroom materials with supportive illustrations for immersion into literacy.
IntelliTools Reading: Balanced Literacy (www.intellitools.com)	Incorporates phonics, guided reading, and comprehension.
The Click to Read Bundle (www.marblesoft.com)	Stories are read with supported illustrations, and students engage in activities that encourage early literacy and comprehension.
Start-to-Finish books (www.donjohnston.com)	Stories are read aloud, and reading comprehension is measured through end-of-story quizzes.

Writing

Software	Skills/Concepts Taught
Co:Writer (www.donjohnston.com)	Word prediction, grammar and vocabulary support that can be added to any word processor or email program.
Write:Outloud (www.donjohnston.com)	Talking word processor that gives immediate speech feedback as students type words, sentences, and paragraphs.
Clicker 5 (www.clicksoft.com)	Lets teachers create word or picture grids on screen that provide support for developing writers.
PixWriter (www.slatersoftware.com)	Picture-assisted writing tool that allows students to engage in writing with teacher-created word/picture banks.
IntelliTools Classroom Suite 4 (www.intellitools.com)	Word processor that allows students to combine graphics, text, and speech to support and enhance writing and communication skills.
Kidspiration (www.inspiration.com)	Helps develop thinking, literacy, and numeracy skills using visual learning principles.

Math

Software	Skills/Concepts Taught
Millie's Math House (www.attainmentcompany.com)	Students explore numbers, shapes, sizes, quantities, patterns, sequencing, addition, and subtraction.
Trudy's Time and Place House (www.attainmentcompany.com)	Activities teach students time-telling skills and explore the concept of time by controlling an animated movie.
Math Pad (www.intellitools.com)	An electronic worksheet allowing students to perform arithmetic directly on the computer.
Counting Coins (www.attainmentcompany.com)	Allows students to sort, match, and purchase from a vending machine with virtual coins
MatchTime (www.attainmentcompany.com)	Students practice basic telling-time exercises.
Money Skills (www.marblesoft.com)	Includes 5 activities that teach counting money and making change.
Show Me Math (www.attainmentcompany.com)	Students practice addition, subtraction, multiplication, and division with the largest number being 20.

Science/Social Studies

Software	Skills/Concepts Taught
Switching on Science (Earth, Habitats, Solar System) (www.softtouch.com)	A standards-based science curriculum especially for students with disabilities. Contains a choice of concrete vocabulary in short-phrase, short-sentence or longer-sentence formats.
Switching on American History (www.softtouch.com)	Accessible history curriculum with three language levels. Units include Biographies, Westward Movement, Colonial Americans, Industrial Revolution and American Symbols.

The following are examples of how an academic goal can be expanded to incorporate software.

Reading	
Original Goal	**Goal with Assistive Technology**
John	
John will read 5 three word phrases that use known words.	John will read 10 complete sentences composed with PixWriter using picture cues to identify at least one novel word per sentence.
Henry	
After listening to a story being read to him, Henry will answer 5 questions about the story.	After using assistive technology to independently read a Start-to-Finish novel, Henry will answer 5 comprehension questions based on the novel.

Writing	
Original Goal	**Goal with Assistive Technology**
Sherry	
Sherry will dictate to a scribe a 10-word note.	Using CoWriter, Sherry will independently create a picture symbol/word note of 10 words or more.
Chuck	
Chuck will choose 5 pictures to put in a journal and dictate a description of the pictures.	Using Clicker 5 and a touch screen, Chuck will independently compose 5 sentences to add to his journal.

Math	
Original Goal	**Goal with Assistive Technology**
David	
David will watch as a peer counts manipulatives in sets of 1 to 10 items.	David will use a math software program with virtual manipulatives and a head switch to choose the correct number of manipulatives that have been counted for sets 1-10.
Matt	
Matt will work on a task for 15 minutes.	Matt will use an online timer to track the amount of time he has worked and press a switch that says "I'm finished" when his time is up.

Chapter 5
Strategies for Alignment

Using a Real-Life Activity to Help Make the Standard Meaningful

Another way for the team to effectively identify target skills for general curriculum access is to address the standards through real-life activities. Although accessing the general curriculum places more emphasis on academics than students with severe disabilities have had in the past, it is still necessary for students to apply these skills in meaningful, real-life contexts. Fortunately, with a little instructional creativity, any state academic standards can be addressed by having students be able to attain and apply skills and knowledge learned in the classroom to real-life situations. The following examples illustrate how academic skills can be embedded in typical daily routines:

- Create a picture symbol homework list (writing)

- Locate a room by its number (math)

- Use a keypad in the cafeteria (math)

- Locate the sports page using newspaper index (reading)

- Follow a picture schedule (reading)

> Accessing the general curriculum places emphasis on academic instruction for students with severe disabilities.
>
> It's your job to make sure these skills are applied in meaningful, real-life contexts.

It is also vital that you consider the age-appropriateness of materials that students use. Generally, for teachers of elementary school children, this is less of a problem. However, even for them, it is important to select age appropriate materials, not materials designed for toddlers. For teachers of students in middle or high school, finding age appropriate materials may be a struggle. Generally, books at a lower reading level are aimed at younger students.

However, there are sets of classic books that have been adapted to lower reading levels (e.g., www.wiesereducational.com).

Also, Don Johnston's Start-to-Finish book series (www.donjohnston.com) includes high interest–low vocabulary books. You may also consider using news magazines that have been written for students (*Time for Kids, Sports Illustrated for Kids*). News-2-You is an internet picture symbol newspaper that comes out weekly and contains information about current events (http://news2you.n2y.com/).

To plan functional activities that give meaning to emerging academic skills, look at the major domains of life, work, home, the community, and leisure settings. It may be helpful to find out some of the activities typical of the students' chronological age in these settings. For example, in a shopping mall, younger students typically accompany adult shoppers but may get to select a toy or food item that the adult purchases. In contrast, middle school students may shop with peers, make their own clothing selection, purchase lunch, and spend money independently. High school students may hold part-time jobs in the mall and help customers with food or clothing purchases.

The following illustrate how academic objectives are made more meaningful by considering the students chronological age and appropriate life environments:

Examples of Real-Life Applications of Geometry Skills

Skill	Home	Work	Leisure	Community
Geometric shapes Age: 7	Play video games that use shapes.	Shape cues for chores at school (e.g., rectangle for toys in toy box; circle for help to set the round table for snack).	Forming shapes while playing games in PE (e.g., Let's make a circle; boys in a line).	Identify shape signs (e.g., stop at red circle sign).
Perimeter and Area Age: 12 (Middle School)	Make a "Where I live" chart showing area of rooms.	Use laser measure to determine perimeter of objects.	Indicate perimeter of playing field to show concept of "out of bounds."	Identify what foods are located in perimeter of grocery store.

Chapter 6
- **Practicing Alignment**
- **Case Study Examples**

Practicing Alignment to State Standards

In earlier chapters, examples were given of how to align objectives to state standards by focusing on ELA and mathematics, incorporating self-determination, using assistive technology, and creating applications for academic skills in the context of real-life activities. Here we provide a suggested practice routine for pulling these ideas together.

Aligning English Language Arts Objectives

Lisa's Scenario

Lisa is a 3rd grade student with Rhett's Syndrome. She is nonverbal and currently uses objects to communicate. She shows an interest in books read to her by peers. She will also sometimes look at pictures in a magazine. Lisa is ambulatory, but has limited use of her hands. She enjoys social contexts and will sometimes make her meaning known by eye gazing or laughing.

In developing a standards-based IEP for Lisa, the team needed to become familiar with the state standards.

The following are some selected standards in each strand of English Language Arts and Ideas for Lisa (Table 6a). The IEP Objectives are shown in Table 6b.

Table 6a

Reading: Literature

Key Ideas and Details	IDEAS for Lisa
Ask and answer questions to demonstrate understanding of a text, referring explicitly to the text as the basis for the answers.	Lisa will answer comprehension questions by using objects/pictures the teacher embeds with the text. (See IEP Objective #3.)
Craft and Structure	
Determine the meaning of words and phrases as they are used in a text, distinguishing literal from nonliteral language.	Lisa will match phrases to definitions for literal and nonliteral text. (See IEP Objective #4.)
Integration of Knowledge and Ideas	
Explain how specific aspects of a text's illustrations contribute to what is conveyed by the words in a story (e.g., create mood, emphasize aspects of a character or setting.)	When told the feeling words "happy," "sad," or "mad," Lisa will choose the picture from the story that matches this word. (See IEP Objective #4.)
Range of Reading and Level of Text Complexity	
By the end of the year, read and comprehend literature, including stories, dramas, and poetry, at the high end of the grades 2–3 text-complexity band independently and proficiently.	Lisa will engage in a read aloud of 3rd grade text by locating the correct page, completing repeated story lines, finding key words, and answering comprehension questions. (See IEP Objective #2.)

Reading: Informational Text

Key Ideas and Details	IDEAS for Lisa
Ask and answer questions to demonstrate understanding of a text, referring explicitly to the text as the basis for the answers	Lisa will generalize her skills in using objects/pictures embedded in text to informational text. (See IEP Objective #3.)
Craft and Structure	
Determine the meaning of general academic and domain-specific words and phrases in a text relevant to a grade 3 topic or subject area.	Lisa will identify meaning of vocabulary words by selecting one to complete a familiar statement. (See IEP Objective #5.)
Integration of Knowledge and Ideas	
Use information gained from illustrations (e.g., maps, photographs) and the words in a text to demonstrate understanding of the text (e.g., where, when, why, and how key events occur.)	Lisa will select the picture that shows "who" and "what" of main events in an article. (See IEP Objective #3.)
Range of Reading and Level of Text Complexity	
By the end of the year, read and comprehend informational texts, including history/social studies, science, and technical texts, at the high end of the grades 2-3 text complexity band independently and proficiently.	Lisa will generalize her skills in read alouds to science and social studies read alouds. (See IEP Objective #3.)

Reading: Foundational Skills

Print Concepts	
No standards in this area for 3rd grade.	
Phonological Awareness	
No standards in this area for 3rd grade.	
Phonics and Word Recognition	**IDEAS for Lisa**
Know and apply grade-level phonics and word analysis skills in decoding words.	Lisa will develop decoding skills through an early phonics program. (See IEP Objective #7.)
Fluency	
Read with sufficient accuracy and fluency to support comprehension.	Lisa will develop independence in read alouds using computer-activated recorded book. (See IEP Objectives #2 and #6.)

Writing

Text Types and Purposes	IDEAS for Lisa
Write opinion pieces on topics or texts, supporting a point of view with reasons.	Lisa will relate one sentence to express a personal opinion and select a reason (e.g., I like ___ because ___). (See IEP Objective #5.)
Production and Distribution of Writing	
With guidance and support from adults, produce writing in which the development and organization are appropriate to task and purpose. (Grade-specific expectations for writing types are defined in standards 1–3 above.)	Lisa will produce and publish one sentence of writing by completing the task analysis to print a sentence she created. (See IEP Objective #6.)
Research to Build and Present Knowledge	
Conduct short research projects that build knowledge about a topic.	Lisa will select a research topic using a picture request and select at least 5 pictures from the internet that provide information about the topic. (See IEP Objective #1.)
Range of Writing	
Write routinely over extended time frames (time for research, reflection, and revision) and shorter time frames (a single sitting or a day or two) for a range of discipline-specific tasks, purposes, and audiences.	Lisa will generalize her sentence generation and printing skills across her academic lessons. (See IEP Objectives #5 and 6.)

Speaking and Listening

Comprehension and Collaboration	IDEAS for Lisa
Engage effectively in a range of collaborative discussions (one-on-one, in groups, and teacher-led) with diverse partners on grade 3 topics and texts, building on others' ideas and expressing one's own clearly.	Lisa will use picture communication in group context and acknowledge others' communication (See IEP Objective #5.)
Report on a topic or text, tell a story, or recount an experience with appropriate facts and relevant, descriptive details, speaking clearly at an understandable pace.	Lisa will give a class report by using sentences generated with picture selections. (See IEP Objective #5.)

Language

Conventions of Standard English	IDEAS for Lisa
Demonstrate command of the conventions of standard English grammar and usage when writing or speaking.	Lisa will generate sentences that follow the conventions of standard English. (See IEP Objective #5.)
Knowledge of Language	
Use knowledge of language and its conventions when writing, speaking, reading, or listening.	Lisa will generalize her sentence generation to communicating with others. (See IEP Objective #5.)
Vocabulary Acquisition and Use	
Determine or clarify the meaning of unknown and multiple-meaning word and phrases based on grade 3 reading and content, choosing flexibly from a range of strategies.	Lisa will use illustrations and context cues when she encounters an unknown word in a read aloud. (See IEP Objective #7.)

Strategy 1: Promote English Language Arts Skills

The team begins by considering the strands of English Language Arts (reading, writing, speaking and listening, language) and the basic components of reading: (phonemic awareness, phonics, comprehension, fluency, and vocabulary). Lisa's state standard is focused on the last three components—comprehension, fluency, and vocabulary. As shown in Table 6a, this team decided to target at least one standard for each component of 3rd grade English Language Arts (most of these components have three or more standards.) It would be a mistake for the IEP team simply to translate these ideas into IEP objectives (i.e., one objective per standard). That would result in about 15 objectives just in this one content area! Instead, they review their ideas to find what skills they imply for Lisa's ongoing growth in ELA.

The team begins by considering the strands of English Language Arts (reading, writing, speaking and listening, language) and the basic components of reading: (Phonemic awareness, phonics, comprehension, fluency, and vocabulary).

Corresponds with Chapter 2, "Promote Broad Skills in English Language Arts and Mathematics," page 35.

Lisa has two challenges in accessing 3rd grade materials in ELA. First, she is a nonreader and, in fact, has only acquired a few foundational skills. She will sit for a read aloud, smile to show some understanding of the story, and look towards an object associated with the story. Second, Lisa has limited hand dexterity. Although she can manipulate objects with some concentrated effort, she will need to rely more on her eye gaze to answer questions. For Lisa's ELA skills to grow, and to target the 3rd grade standards, she especially needs to learn to:

1. Answer "who" and "what" comprehension questions during read alouds of both narrative and informational texts.

2. Identify pictures that relate to key themes, convey emotion, or illustrate new vocabulary.

3. Expand her vocabulary to include words from 3rd grade literature.

4. Develop independence in using technology for read alouds as well as responding to peer/adult readers.

5. Fill in written sentences by choosing pictures/objects to dictate her response and then independently print these.

6. Develop a picture communication system and generalize this to group discussions and class presentations.

7. Develop beginning reading skills through instruction in decoding.

These seven priorities make a more reasonable list for Lisa's IEP. By applying some additional strategies, they can be further developed to be effective and meaningful for Lisa. The team considers self-determination next.

Strategy 2:
Promote Self-Determination

Lisa sometimes becomes passive, looking at activities of others but not engaging in tasks herself. One way Lisa's team could generate ideas to help her access the 3rd grade English Language Arts standards is to incorporate self-determination practices.

Corresponds with Chapter 3, "Focus on Self-Determination," page 57.

The skills targeted for Lisa are ambitious. The IEP team hopes she will grow from relying mostly on nonsymbolic communication (smiling and some vocalizing) and some picture gazing, to answering questions with these pictures and using them for communication. One way to motivate Lisa to move forward with her use of picture communication will be to build in her preferences. Lisa also can use her emerging ELA skills to become more independent in her own learning.

1. Lisa will choose books to be read aloud during individual reading times.

2. Lisa will independently engage with books using technology for read alouds.

3. Lisa will initiate use of picture communication for requests.

Strategy 3:
Use Assistive Technology

Lisa especially needs access to more assistive technology. While she can learn to answer comprehension questions by eye gazing across an array of pictures or objects, she also needs to develop a means to initiate responding. Her newly emerging picture communication can be combined with some type of technology, including a touch screen or switch and voice output. This technology can also increase her options for accessing literature.

As Lisa's team reviews her objectives; they note that many will provide her with skills that will assist her in completing other activities in her daily routine. They decide to expand some of these objectives by adding in the use of AAC to further address instruction in English Language Arts instruction as well as skills in her daily routine.

Corresponds with Chapter 4, "Using Assistive Technology," page 63.

1. Lisa will use a voice output device with picture symbols to communicate requests.

2a. Given two pictures presented on a voice output device or computer touch screen, Lisa will answer "what" and "who" comprehension questions.

2b. Given two pictures presented on a voice output device or computer touch screen, Lisa will select one to fill in a sentence.

3. Lisa will use a touch screen computer to print a sentence she composed or activate a recorded book.

Strategy 4:
Embed in Real Life Activities

To make sure these IEP objectives are meaningful to Lisa, the team discusses how they can be used within the context of her daily routines as well as during English Language Arts. They come up with these ideas:

Lisa's team notes that her objectives are designed to provide her with skills that can be used in daily routines as well as ELA. Next, they discuss how the skills can be used specifically to address daily routines.

Corresponds with Chapter 5, "Using a Real-Life Activity to Help Make the Standard Meaningful, *page 73*.

- Lisa can use pictures for requesting during lunch and break times as well as during class times.

- During times when the class chooses literature for independent reading, Lisa can have options that relate to her special interests, which are horses and swimming, as well as other stories from the 3rd grade reading list. The teacher may begin with some literature on these topics to teach her how to answer comprehension questions.

- Lisa can be taught to generalize her "who" and "what" answers and sentence writing to compose daily reports to share with her family about her day.

- Lisa can also generalize her emerging ELA skills to social stories the teacher will use to help her learn skills needed for the school environment, like how to eat in the cafeteria.

Putting It All Together:
Lisa's 3rd Grade IEP Objectives in English Language Arts

After considering the four strategies, the IEP team sets the following IEP objectives for English Language Arts. Notice that these objectives do not restate the standards, but target the skills Lisa needs to access the standards. Refer back to Table 6a to see how these objectives are cross-referenced to the standards. Each of the "Ideas for Lisa" in Table 6a has a number. These numbers correspond with the IEP objective shown below that helps Lisa learn this standard. The IEP team would follow a similar process to complete Lisa's IEP in other target areas.

Table 6b

IEP Objectives in English Language Arts

1. Lisa will select a research topic using a picture request and copy/paste at least 5 pictures from the internet to create a report about the topic. (Writing Standard 3.7)

2. Lisa will participate in read-alouds (1:1 or whole class) by finding each page, pointing to illustrations, completing a sentence and answering a recall question for 4 out of 5 narrative or informational passages. (Reading: Literature, Standard 3.10; Reading: Foundational Skills, Standard 3.4)

3. When given pictures/objects embedded with passages that are adapted from 3rd grade narrative and informational texts, Lisa will use these pictures/objects to answer "who" and "what" questions about the main ideas for 8 out of 10 questions per passage. (Reading: Literature, Standard 3.1; Reading: Informational Text, Standards 3.1, 3.7, 3.10)

4. Lisa will identify at least 40 new picture vocabulary words or phrases (10 per quarter) that are presented in the context of adapted 3rd grade text and include feeling words, story component words (e.g., "author"), nonliteral phrases, and other key terms. (Reading: Literature, Standard 3.4 and 3.7; Reading: Informational Text, Standard 3.4)

5. Lisa will apply her new picture vocabulary to fill in sentence templates (I like___; ___(who)___(did what); This story was about ___) for 7 out of 8 trials. She will generalize these sentences to at least three formats including written reports, peer group discussions, and a class presentation.(Reading: Informational Text, Standard 3.4; Writing, Standards 3.1 and 3.10; Speaking and Listening, Standards 3.1 and 3.4; Language, Standards 3.1 and 3.3)

6. Lisa will create written essays/reports by selecting pictures/phrases, using cut/paste icons to put them in a document, and printing them for at least 4 reports. (Reading: Foundational Skills, Standard 3.4; Writing, Standard 3.4 and 3.10)

7. Lisa will analyze new words by recognizing initial consonant sounds, text illustrations, and other context cues. (Reading: Foundational Skills, Standard 3.3; Language, Standard 3.4)

Aligning Mathematics Objectives

Jerome's Scenario

Jerome is a student with Down Syndrome and a moderate intellectual disability. He has mastered about 50 sight words and is learning to apply them in activities of daily living. Jerome also has learned to recognize initial and final consonants and short vowels, and can decode many simple words. With his sight words and decoding skills, he can often help the teacher read short passages of text that have been prepared with controlled vocabulary. He communicates using a picture wallet and single spoken words to make requests, answer questions, and socialize. In math, he rote counts from 1-10, but cannot count objects consistently or recognize numbers consistently. Jerome does understand the purpose of money and likes to make purchases, but needs help counting out the correct number of dollars. Jerome is 11 years old and in 6th grade.

In developing a standards-based IEP for Jerome, the team needed to become familiar with the state standards.

The following are some selected standards in each strand of Mathematics and ideas for Jerome (Table 6c). The IEP Objectives are shown in Table 6d.

Table 6c

Selected 6th Grade Common Core State Standards Mathematics

Ratios and Proportional Relationships 6.RP	
Understand ratio concepts and use ratio reasoning to solve problems.	**Ideas for Jerome**
Understand the concept of a ratio and use ratio language to describe a ratio relationship between two quantities. *For example, "The ratio of wings to beaks in the birdhouse at the zoo was 2:1, because for every 2 wings there was 1 beak." "For every vote candidate A received, candidate C received nearly three votes."*	Apply the concept of ratio to planning a trip. For example, for every one car that we have, we can transport 4 students. If we have 8 students in the class, how many cars would it take to transport all the students? What if there were 12 students? 16 students? Let Jerome use a graphic organizer to plan his answer. (See IEP Objective #1.)
The Number System 6.NS	
Apply and extend previous understandings of multiplication and division to divide fractions by fractions.	
Interpret and compute quotients of fractions, and solve word problems involving division of fractions by fractions, e.g., by using visual fraction models and equations to represent the problem. *For example, create a story context for (2/3) ÷ (3/4) and use a visual fraction model to show the quotient; use the relationship between multiplication and division to explain that (2/3) ÷ (3/4) = 8/9 because 3/4 of 8/9 is 2/3. (In general, (a/b) ÷ (c/d) = ad/bc.) How much chocolate will each person get if 3 people share 1/2 lb of chocolate equally? How many 3/4-cup servings are in 2/3 of a cup of yogurt? How wide is a rectangular strip of land with length 3/4 mi and area 1/2 square mi?*	To do this skill, Jerome will work with fractions that are easily divided. For example, given a serving size of ½ a pizza, how many servings are in 2½ pizzas? (See IEP Objective #1.)
Compute fluently with multi-digit numbers and find common factors and multiples.	
Fluently add, subtract, multiply, and divide multi-digit decimals using the standard algorithm for each operation.	Jerome will use a calculator to add, subtract, multiply or divide by entering each digit of the number and selecting the correct symbol (+, -, /, x) and =. In applying this skill, Jerome will become more fluent in number recognition. (See IEP Objective #2.)

Selected 6th Grade Common Core State Standards Mathematics

Apply and extend previous understandings of numbers to the system of rational numbers.	Ideas for Jerome
Understand that positive and negative numbers are used together to describe quantities having opposite directions or values (e.g., temperature above/below zero, elevation above/below sea level, credits/debits, positive/negative electric charge); use positive and negative numbers to represent quantities in real-world contexts, explaining the meaning of 0 in each situation.	In math stories about spending, Jerome will express a balance of money as positive, negative (in debt), or zero. (See IEP Objective #4.)
Solve real-world and mathematical problems by graphing points in all four quadrants of the coordinate plane. Include use of coordinates and absolute value to find distances between points with the same first coordinate or the same second coordinate.	Jerome will graph points on a plane (x,y). This skill can be applied to real-life activities like locating a store on a map of a mall (See IEP Objective #5.)
Expressions and Equations 6.EE	
Apply and extend previous understandings of arithmetic to algebraic expressions.	
Write expressions that record operations with numbers and with letters standing for numbers. *For example, express the calculation, "Subtract y from 5" as 5 – y.*	After hearing a math story, Jerome will write the problem to be solved using numbers and letters (e.g., 5 - x = 10). (See IEP Objective #3.)
Reason about and solve one-variable equations and inequalities.	
Understand solving an equation or inequality as a process of answering a question: Which values from a specified set, if any, make the equation or inequality true? Use substitution to determine whether a given number in a specified set makes an equation or inequality true.	Given an equation and a list of numbers, Jerome will attempt to solve the equations to determine which equations are true. (See IEP Objective #3.)
Represent and analyze quantitative relationships between dependent and independent variables.	
Use variables to represent two quantities in a real-world problem that change in relationship to one another; write an equation to express one quantity, thought of as the dependent variable, in terms of the other quantity, thought of as the independent variable. Analyze the relationship between the dependent and independent variables using graphs and tables, and relate these to the equation. *For example, in a problem involving motion at constant speed, list and graph ordered pairs of distances and times, and write the equation d = 65t to represent the relationship between distance and time.*	Jerome will complete a table related to spending to show how the total purchase price changes depending on the numbers of items purchased (e.g., How does the total purchase price of tickets change as the number of tickets purchased changes?) (See IEP Objective #6.)

Strategy 1: Promote Mathematics Skills

The basic components of mathematics are computation, measurement, geometry, patterns/algebra, and data analysis/graphing. The 6th grade standards focus on ratios and proportional relationships, number sense, and expressions and equations as shown in Table 6c. The IEP team looked at one or two priority standards in each of these areas based on the recommendation of the math teacher (in the full CCSS there are about four to five 6th grade standards in each area). They then brainstormed skills for Jerome that would link to these standards. The challenge for Jerome is that he has few mathematics skills. He does not yet perform any computation and is inconsistent in number identification. The team targets the goal of promoting Jerome's computation and number recognition concurrent with these other skills. Jerome's strength is that he likes to set up and pass out materials. By using hands-on materials, he may be able to learn some of the mathematics concepts. The following are a tentative list of skills the team made after working from the Common Core State Standards in Mathematics for 6th grade:

> The team begins by considering the 6th grade standards of Mathematics (ratios and proportional relationships, number sense, and expressions and equations).
>
> Corresponds with Chapter 2 Promoting Broad Skills in ELA and Mathematics, beginning on page 35.

1. Jerome will divide materials into sets. He will select the number of items in each set. When these numbers are fractional, ratios, or exceed 10, he will use a graphic organizer. For example, to identify a fraction, he would use a graphic to identify (how many are in part of the set/how many are in the whole).

Note: By manipulating items into sets and then matching these sets to the written number, Jerome will build his numeracy skills. To make these skills align with the grade level, some of these sets will be based on fractions and ratios, but Jerome will fill in a graphic organizer to help him with expressing these more complex concepts.

2. Jerome will identify numbers 1-9, computation symbols, and = sign on a calculator while performing computation.

Note: Jerome might also do some work with flash cards to become fluent in number identification. By applying his number recognition skills to using a calculator, Jerome can work on grade-aligned math problems.

3. Jerome will use letters to stand in for unknown numbers in an equation.

Note: Because Jerome is learning to create sets and find a number symbol that identifies the set, it may be possible to teach him the concept of a "mystery" or unknown value. For example, the teacher might put "x" number of manipulatives in a closed shoebox and have him put an "x" on the box because he does not yet know how many are in the box.

4. Jerome will create a simple linear equation (e.g., $9 - x = 5$) to summarize a math story and then compute the solution.

Note: After Jerome has the concept of the unknown value and has begun to do some set combinations, he can begin to summarize these actions as equations. This might be shaped by having him fill in one variable, then more than one, balance the sets, etc.

5. Jerome will use positive and negative numbers (up to 10) and zero to indicate monetary balances.

Note: Jerome already understands money. If the teacher uses a token economy, class store, or lessons on purchasing, Jerome can be given the opportunity to count out $1 bills to build his mathematics skills. If he is allowed to borrow money for items beyond his means, or spend all he has, he can learn the concept of negative numbers and zero (no money).

6. Jerome will find the point on a plane using maps of familiar locations and then generalize this to a coordinate plane.

Note: This skill can be scaffolded by beginning with simple maps and then made more abstract by using an actual coordinate plane. Once Jerome can recognize numbers, he may be able to learn the skill of finding a point on a coordinate plane (e.g., 2,4).

7. Jerome will use a table to find out the cost of buying duplicate items.

Note: Using stories about purchases, Jerome can learn to find out how much he would spend for multiple sets of the same item by referring to a table. For example, if he wants 4 tickets to a $10 movie, that would be $40. This table will also give Jerome an opportunity to learn to read numbers higher than 9 and to count by 5s and 10s.

Strategy 2:
Promote Self-Determination

Mathematics provides an excellent opportunity for self-determination because a student may apply math skills to self-monitor behavior (I raised my hand 2 times), self-evaluate progress towards a goal (goal is 10; I did 8); set a goal (e.g., complete 5 math problems today), and problem solve (how much money is needed to take a friend to lunch). Jerome has not had much success in math to date. His current numeracy skills are far below the types of activities his 6th grade classmates will be performing. Building in some self-determination skills can help Jerome approach new challenging tasks with some decision-making. Here are some examples of what the IEP team discussed for Jerome.

> The team identifies ways to promote Jerome's self-determination while working on his math skills.
>
> Corresponds with Chapter 3, "Focus on Self-Determination," *page 57.*

- When presenting a math word problem, Jerome could choose the numbers to use in that day's problem. He could also choose which manipulatives to put into sets.

- As Jerome masters using a graphic organizer, he can more easily self-direct his learning. He can learn to say, then do, the steps to solve the problem.

- Jerome might set a goal for how many math problems to try that day. He could count and graph the number completed. This self-monitoring and self-evaluation also promotes his emerging mathematics skills.

- Jerome can select which letter he wants to use that day for the unknown number (e.g., x, z, q, t).

- Jerome is learning problem-solving each time he finds the answer to a real-world math problem (e.g., how to divide the pencils across work groups).

By considering the use of assistive technology, more options become available for how Jerome will practice and demonstrate math skills.

Corresponds with Chapter 4, Using Assistive Technology.

Strategy 3:
Use Assistive Technology

Now the team looks at the exact responses that will be used for Jerome to demonstrate mastery of each math concept. By considering the use of assistive technology, more options become available for how Jerome will practice and demonstrate these skills.

1. The calculator is an important form of assistive technology for Jerome. Once he learns to enter numbers on the calculator, he will be able to perform more of the problems from the 6th grade text. Once he can find the numbers 1-9, the operation symbols, and equals sign, he will be able to compute problems.

2. Many of the skills Jerome needs to acquire can be practiced on the computer. For example, he could move items on a touch screen to create sets or perform computation on an on-screen calculator.

3. The graphic organizers Jerome will learn to use are also a form of assistive technology. For example, he will have a graphic organizer to help him write fractions as ___ (how many are in part of the set)/___ (how many are in the whole).

4. Jerome might also benefit from use of a number line that includes negative numbers to help him learn the concept of positive and negative numbers and zero.

Strategy 4:
Embed in Real-Life Activities

Given that Jerome is in middle school, it is especially important that his emerging math skills have utility in his daily life. While some of Jerome's instructional activities may be using traditional math materials, others may be embedded in the context of familiar routines. The following show how the team adapted the objectives or planned instructional applications to make the objectives meaningful and relevant for Jerome. Here are some of the ideas the IEP team had for Jerome.

> Some of Jerome's instructional activities may be embedded in the context of familiar routines. The team adapted the objectives or planned instructional applications to make the objectives applicable to real-life situations for Jerome.
>
> Corresponds with Chapter 5, Using a Real-Life Activity.

1. Jerome can divide materials for projects into sets for the class or his small group, and use this experience to practice matching numbers to sets and creating fractions and ratios.

2. By having a class store or token economy, Jerome can apply his general knowledge of money and interest in purchasing to practice counting accurately and learning the concept of debt (negative numbers) and zero (no money).

3. Identifying points on a plane can become very meaningful when applied to planning a route through a neighborhood or store.

4. Jerome might practice using the calculator to add a list of purchases or a simple budget.

5. Math word problems that yield equations can come from situations familiar to Jerome. For example, if you have 4 cans of soda and 6 friends coming to visit, how many more sodas are needed? ($4 + x = 6$)

Putting it All Together:
Jerome's 6th Grade IEP Objectives in Mathematics

After reviewing the standards together and Jerome's needs in the area of mathematics, then considering ways to use self-determination, assistive technology, and real-life scenarios to teach these skills, the IEP team developed Jerome's objectives. Look back at Table 6c to see how each of these relates to the 6th grade standards.

Table 6d

Jerome's 6th Grade IEP Objectives in Mathematics

1. When given a cluster of up to 20 objects, Jerome will divide them into 1-5 sets and identify the number that represents each set for 8 of 10 trials. He will subdivide these sets to show division of fractions and ratios and represent these numbers using a graphic organizer for 8 of 10 trials. (Mathematics: Rations and Proportional Relationships, Standard 6.1; Number System, Standard 6.1)

2. When given math problems with up to three digits, Jerome will follow the steps of a task analysis to use a calculator to enter each number, the operation, and the equals sign, and then record the answer on his worksheet with 9 of 10 problems correct. (Number System, Standard 6.3)

3. When given an unknown in a math word problem, Jerome will designate the unknown number as a letter and complete an equation statement for 8 of 10 stories. He will then use his calculator or a number line to solve for the unknown with 8 of 10 problems correct. (Expressions and Equations, Standards 6.2a and 6.5)

4. Jerome will count his dollars from the class token economy/class store and then write positive and negative numbers to 20, including 0, to correctly state his balance on 9 of 10 days. (Number System, Standard 6.5)

5. Jerome will locate point x, y on a coordinate plane for 4 of 5 trials and generalize this skill to locating a point on a map. (Number System, Standard 6.8)

6. Jerome will use a table to determine the cost of a set of items that have the same price (e.g., 3 items at $5) for 4 of 5 trials and create a statement for 8 of 10 word problems. He will then use his calculator or a number line to solve for the unknown with 8 of 10 problems correct. (Expressions and Equations, Standard 9)

Case Study Example

Carina's Scenario

Carina is a 5th grade student with severe multiple disabilities. She uses a wheelchair and has limited movement in her left arm. She can move her head from side to side. Carina uses a head switch to greet teachers and peers. She smiles when listening to stories that are read to her by an adult. Carina does not recognize any math symbols and does not respond to teacher countdowns. Using the five guidelines from Chapter 1, Carina's IEP team will develop priority standards in academic content areas as well as other important areas that Carina needs to work on. Once the priority standards are developed, the IEP team will develop objectives that make the standards accessible for Carina.

> Using the five guidelines from Chapter 1, Carina's IEP team will develop priority standards in academic content areas as well as other important areas that Carina needs to work on.

Guidelines to Select IEP Goals that Promote Alignment	How Carina's IEP Team will Follow the Guidelines
Guideline One: Become Familiar with State Standards	Carina's assigned grade is 5th grade. The general education teacher who is a part of Carina's IEP team is an experienced 5th grade teacher who is familiar with grade-level standards in English Language Arts, Mathematics, Science, and Social Studies. Carina's state uses the Common Core State Standards in English Language Arts and Mathematics. Carina's IEP team is using the state's curriculum and the school system's pacing guide to become familiar with grade-level appropriate academic goals.
Guideline Two: Become Familiar with the State's Approach to Extending State Standards	Carina's state provides a curricular framework for the Common Core State Standards for students who take the alternate assessment. The team obtains copies of these frameworks. These help the team to determine what standards are priorities.

Guidelines to Select IEP Goals that Promote Alignment	How Carina's IEP Team will Follow the Guidelines
Guideline Three: Keep the Planning Student-Focused	Each member of Carina's IEP team is contributing information about Carina based on current assessments. Carina's teacher reports that Carina is using her switch to greet people and smiles when books are being read to her, or when music is playing. She has begun to show some recognition of the stories by laughing at familiar lines and will touch an object that goes with the story. In math, she will help put objects in sets by dropping objects into boxes, but does not yet seem to know what these sets represent. Carina has also shown a lot of interest during science class. When asked, she will look at the material that represents the concept (e.g., "Carina, look at our model of a rock formation"). Carina's Occupational Therapist reports that Carina is beginning to make progress touching a switch with her left hand. Carina's Physical Therapist reports that Carina is assisting with the shifting of her body weight when she is being lifted. Carina's Speech/Language Therapist notes that Carina is pointing to herself when her name is called. She also has begun to identify a range of familiar objects (e.g., Find the ball) and occasionally to use them to make a request (e.g., Play ball). Carina's parents report that she is verbalizing a sound like "Mom" when she sees her mother. She is also reaching toward toys and books that she wants at home. She chooses books most often.
Guideline Four: Consider Both Specific Academic Goals and Broad Access Goals	Carina's IEP team plans Carina's goals in four academic content areas (English Language Arts, Mathematics, Science, and Social Studies) that are part of the 5th grade curriculum. However, the team also determines that Carina's IEP should address other goals that are important for Carina, such as therapy goals, leisure goals, and daily living skills.
Guideline Five: Ask the Question, "Is It Really Academics (English Language Arts, Math, Science, Social Studies)?"	Carina's IEP team spent some time with the state standards brainstorming what Carina might do using a similar approach to the examples shown in Tables 6a and 6c for Lisa and Jerome. Carina's case is challenging because her current academic skills are so far from the grade-level expectations. In contrast, the committee decides she has some important emerging skills that can promote academic learning. She is beginning to look at the key materials in a lesson. She has begun asking for an activity using an object. She can manipulate materials. She also has begun to get the big idea of a text by associating it with an object after several readings. In English Language Arts she needs to comprehend more aspects of text that are adapted from the 5th grade literature. In math, she can create sets to begin building mathematic concepts. She might use picture symbols combined with mathematic symbols for now to bridge understanding.

After Carina's IEP team has decided on priority academic goals for Carina, they develop objectives for each goal.

In order to be sure that the IEP objectives are creating access to state standards, the team uses the following four strategies:

• Select skills that promote overall English Language Arts and mathematics skills

• Focus on self-determination skills

• Use assistive technology to increase active, independent responding

• Use real-life activities to give meaning to the academic concept

Standard	IEP Objectives	Strategies Used for Alignment
5th Grade **English Language Arts:** **Reading: Literature** Determine a theme of a story, drama, or poem from details in the text, including how characters in a story or drama respond to challenges, or how the speaker in a poem reflects upon a topic; summarize the text. **Reading: Informational Text** Determine two or more main ideas of a text and explain how they are supported by key details; summarize the text. **Carina's priority goal:** Carina will identify objects/pictures that indicate the theme of the literature that is read to her.	Given two choices of objects/symbols that represent the main idea found in a story adapted from the 5th grade literature, Carina will touch the object/symbol requested on 4 out of 5 opportunities. She will generalize this skill to a poem, an informational passage, and a drama.	**Promote broad ELA skills:** Carina is learning to identify objects/symbols, a pre-literacy skill. **Focus on self-determination:** Carina will sometimes choose the text that is being read to her. She will also report to the teacher whether she liked or disliked the text. **Use assistive technology to increase active, independent responding:** Carina can use a computer program that scans through choices of symbols she has to choose from. When the symbol she thinks is correct is highlighted, Carina will use her head switch to stop the scan and make a choice. Carina will also activate one of two switches that state "I like this story," or "I do not like this story." **Use real-life activities to give meaning to the academic concept:** This goal can be expanded to include books that highlight objects/symbols that Carina will use every day, such as names of important people, places in Carina's community, or common household or school objects that she likes to use.

Standard	IEP Objectives	Strategies Used for Alignment
Writing: Produce clear and coherent writing in which the development and organization are appropriate to task, purpose, and audience. Write opinion pieces on topics or texts, supporting a point of view with reasons and information. **Carina's priority goal:** Carina will dictate sentences to a scribe and select an illustration to accompany the sentence that shows understanding of the sentence.	Given a writing template including three sentences to fill in, Carina will select objects/pictures and use an adjective to dictate to a scribe how to complete the sentences for 4 of 5 writing opportunities. She will demonstrate understanding of her writing by creating or selecting an illustration for it. For example, I like____ (object choice) Because it is_____ (adjective choice) And it is ____ (adjective choice)	**Promote broad ELA skills:** Carina is creating sentences and demonstrating comprehension of the sentences she has created. This expands her overall ELA skills by increasing her symbol vocabulary. **Focus on self-determination:** Carina will select the objects/pictures and also the adjective to describe the pictures. (choice-making). She could also determine the resources she will use to find appropriate pictures (e.g., magazines, clip art, etc.) (decision-making). **Use assistive technology to increase active, independent responding:** Carina is using simple forms of assistive technology by using objects and pictures. She could also choose her illustrations from a computer program (e.g., Boardmaker) or an Internet source (e.g., Google images). **Use real-life activities to give meaning to the academic concept:** This goal can be expanded to include topics that relate to pre-vocational activities, such as choosing after-school jobs. Carina could explore jobs through community-based instructional programs and compose sentences about each job that interests her, indicating why she would or would not like that job.

Standard	IEP Objectives	Strategies Used for Alignment
Communication Report on a topic or text or present an opinion, sequencing ideas logically and using appropriate facts and relevant, descriptive details to support main ideas or themes; speak clearly at an understandable pace. Engage effectively in a range of collaborative discussions (one-on-one, in groups, and teacher-led) with diverse partners on grade 5 topics and texts, building on others' ideas and expressing her own clearly. **Carina's priority goal:** Carina will use voice output devices to communicate preferences and academic content.	Carina will present her written product in front of the class and in a small group by using a switch-activated voice output device on 4 of 5 opportunities. She will generalize this skill to at least 5 different topics. Carina will communicate a request or preference using a picture symbol for at least 4 of 5 opportunities. She will generalize this skill not only to personal needs (e.g., wanting a drink), but also to small group class projects (e.g., wanting a turn with the science materials).	**Promote broad ELA skills:** Carina is communicating on a topic and within the context of the class and a small group. **Focus on self-determination:** Carina is communicating her preferences (choice-making). After her presentation is complete, Carina could also rate her own performance (self-evaluation). **Use assistive technology to increase active, independent responding:** Carina is using an AAC device to present her written product. She is also using pictures symbols to communicate preferences and requests. **Use real-life activities to give meaning to the academic concept:** This goal can be expanded to include leisure opportunities. Carina could request to take a turn or be on a specific team during an after-school club activity.

Standard	IEP Objectives	Strategies Used for Alignment
5th Grade Mathematics **Operations and Algebraic Thinking** Write simple expressions that record calculations with numbers, and interpret numerical expressions without evaluating them. For example, express the calculation "add 8 and 7, then multiply by 2" as 2 × (8 + 7). Recognize that 3 × (18932 + 921) is three times as large as 18932 + 921, without having to calculate the indicated sum or product.	Carina will create equations by putting objects in equal sets on a graphic organizer and matching a number for 8 of 10 equations that add to 10. For example: $6 = 2 \times (2 + 1)$ $\begin{matrix} \bullet\bullet\bullet \\ \bullet\bullet\bullet \end{matrix} = \begin{matrix} \bullet\bullet \\ \bullet\bullet \end{matrix} \quad \begin{matrix} \bullet \\ \bullet \end{matrix}$ $6 \quad = \quad 6$	**Promote broad mathematics skills:** Carina is learning to identify numbers and count sets. **Focus on self-determination:** Carina could choose the appropriate graphic organizer needed to solve her problem (problem-solving). **Use assistive technology to increase active, independent responding:** Carina is using simple forms of assistive technology by using graphic organizers. She could also use virtual manipulatives and a touch screen computer to solve the same problems. **Use real-life activities to give meaning to the academic concept:** This goal can be expanded to include solving the equation that is set in the context of a real world scenario. For example, Carina could solve equations that relate to the amount of money needed for a family to go to the movies (e.g., 4 x bus fare + movie ticket).

Standard	IEP Objectives	Strategies Used for Alignment
Numbers & Operations in Base Ten Recognize that in a multi-digit number, a digit in one place represents 10 times as much as it represents in the place to its right and 1/10 of what it represents in the place to its left. **Carina's priority goal:** Carina will use graphic organizers to solve 5th grade math problems	Carina will place base ten manipulatives on a place value mat to represent 2 digit numbers (4 of 5 representations correct).	**Promote broad mathematics skills:** Carina is learning counting and place value skills. **Focus on self-determination:** Carina could choose the numbers she would like to represent (choice-making). She could also use similar manipulatives to monitor daily activities completed (self-management). **Use assistive technology to increase active, independent responding:** Carina could use virtual manipulatives and a touch screen to complete the math lesson.. **Use real life activities to give meaning to the academic concept:** The self-management strategy can be combined with a real-life activity. Carina can keep track of activities completed with "ones" blocks on a place value mat. When she completes 10 activities, she will replace the "ones" block with a "tens" block.

Standard	IEP Objectives	Strategies Used for Alignment
Numbers & Operations-Fractions Interpret a fraction as division of the numerator by the denominator ($a/b = a \div b$). Solve word problems involving division of whole numbers leading to answers in the form of fractions or mixed numbers, e.g., by using visual fraction models or equations to represent the problem. **Carina's priority goal:** Carina will work with a partner or group to determine the numerator and denominator in fractions to solve real word problems	Carina will use fractional parts (e.g., a square divided into fourths) and a graphic organizer to determine if the parts are more, less, or equal to a whole for 4 of 5 problems. For example: 	**Promote broad mathematics skills:** Carina is learning to identify numbers and use fractions. **Focus on self-determination:** Carina will choose the item to be divided within the context of a word problem (choice-making). Carina could also determine how many parts are needed to divide among a group of peers (problem-solving). **Use assistive technology to increase active, independent responding:** Carina will use virtual manipulatives to represent her fractions. **Use real-life activities to give meaning to the academic concept:** During a class party, Carina will determine what fraction of a pizza or pie she would like.

Standard	IEP Objectives	Strategies Used for Alignment
Geometry Represent real world and mathematical problems by graphing points in the first quadrant of the coordinate plane, and interpret coordinate values of points in the context of the situation. **Carina's priority goal:** Carina will find points on a plane to solve real world problems.	Carina will find points on a plane by locating and matching locations on illustrated maps (e.g., point a,b is the location of the library in the school or point 2,3 is where she sits in class row 2, seat 3).	**Promote broad mathematics skills:** Carina is learning to identify points on a plane. **Focus on self-determination:** Carina will set a goal to determine how many points of the map she will locate (goal-setting). Carina will determine if the points on the maps she has located are of interest to her (e.g., I would like to go to the library. I would not like to go to the office; self-awareness). **Use assistive technology to increase active, independent responding:** Carina will use an interactive map of the city that she lives in. **Use real-life activities to give meaning to the academic concept:** Carina will use the map to determine where she and her friends live in the community.

Standard	IEP Objectives	Strategies Used for Alignment
5th Grade Science Discuss and determine the role of light, temperature, and soil composition in an ecosystem's capacity to support life. Identify and analyze forces that cause change in landforms over time including water and ice; wind; and gravity. Investigate the water cycle including the processes of: • evaporation • condensation • precipitation • run-off **Carina's priority goal:** Carina will use picture symbols and models to answer questions about 5th grade science concepts.	Carina will identify that plants need sunlight, soil, and water, and indicate what happens when plants freeze for 2 of 3 opportunities. Carina will show on a model what happens when wind and water erode a landform for 2 of 3 opportunities. Carina will match picture symbols for condensation and evaporation to cold ("sweating") and hot ("steaming") beverages for 2 of 3 opportunities.	**Promote broad ELA or mathematics skills:** Carina is learning to identify picture symbols (an early ELA skill). **Focus on self-determination:** Carina will determine (weekly) which source (e.g., water, light, soil) is needed to maintain the growth of the plants in her classroom (problem-solving). Carina will determine if a liquid is too hot to drink based on the steam coming from the cup (decision-making). **Use assistive technology to increase active, independent responding:** Carina will use the Internet to explore different models of eroded landforms. **Use real-life activities to give meaning to the academic concept:** Carina will help to maintain a classroom garden by observing and determining the basic needs of the plants in the garden, and by communicating to teacher or peer what the plants need using picture symbols.

Standard	IEP Objectives	Strategies Used for Alignment
5th Grade Social Studies Analyze major documents that formed the foundations of the American idea of constitutional government. Locate and describe people of diverse ethnic and religious cultures, past and present, in the United States. **Carina's priority goal:** Carina will identify objects that represent historical ideas and cultural groups.	Carina will select object that represents main idea of informational text from 4 of 5 passages read aloud that reflect at least 3 different Early American documents. Carina will sort cultural items used with read alouds into same/different for 4 of 5 objects.	**Promote broad ELA or mathematics skills:** Carina is learning to identify objects that represent concepts (an early literacy skill). **Focus on self-determination:** Carina will identify her cultural background and objects related to it (self-awareness). **Use assistive technology to increase active, independent responding:** Carina will use reading software that scans and reads adapted informational text aloud. **Use real-life activities to give meaning to the academic concept:** Carina will work with her parents to create a report about her own cultural background that she can share with other family members and peers.

Chapter 7

Teaching to the Standards

While planning the IEP is important, students will be unlikely to master these goals unless they receive effective instruction. This effective instruction will include procuring assistive technology and adapting materials, creating both a method for progress monitoring and opportunities for the student to learn the responses using systematic prompting and fading.

Using Assistive Technology to "Show What they Know"

When learning academic content, students will need some means to "show what they know." If students have an existing communication system (e.g., voice output system with pictures), it will be important to add additional symbols needed for the content area. For example, in math, students will need symbols like +, -, >, =. In science, students may need words like "precipitation" and "life cycle." For social studies, they may need symbols for historical figures like Harriet Tubman and Abraham Lincoln. In English Language Arts, they will need pictures for the characters in the story and major themes and events (e.g., hurricane). Sometimes it may be most efficient to create response boards specifically for the selected academic unit. For example, a **response board** in science for a unit about biology. (*Figure 1*)

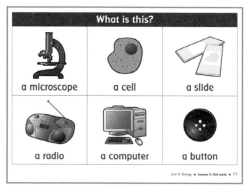

Figure 1. Teaching to Standards Science page.

In addition to a response board, students need a mode of communication. Some students use speech and can generate answers to questions. Many students with severe disabilities will need to use a response board and some nonvocal means of responding. This may include pointing to one of the responses on the board. Students may need some instruction to learn how to make a pointing response. These pointing responses may be especially effective when paired with a voice output device. *Figure 2* shows the **GoTalk** device that can be programmed with pictures from any content area.

Other students may not have adequate motor control to point, but may be able to identify a response using an eye gaze. The teacher might cut apart the response board and affix the symbols to a cardboard or Plexiglas "windowpane" with one symbol in each corner. The teacher then watches the student to see which item is selected by looking at it for several seconds. Students may need instruction to learn to hold their gaze on one selection (e.g., "The answer is 'rain.' Look at the picture of 'rain' right here. Keep looking so I know this is your answer. Good looking!") Sometimes it may

Figure 2. GoTalk 9+

help the eye gazer to highlight the correct response by framing it with a bright color border and then removing the border once the student knows the correct answer. Some students may not be able to point, but may be able to select the response by pulling it off. Pictures may be velcroed in place and then pulled by the student.

Sometimes the response is more than one word. The student may be asked to read a repeated story line or use a complete sentence. *Figure 3* technology can be used for programming longer student responses.

Figure 3. GoTalk 32+

Remember, it is up to you as the teacher to provide your students with the opportunities to make active, independent responses. Be creative and think about how you will increase your students' ability to communicate by using technology and challenging students to communicate more!

Adapting Books and Other Printed Materials

General educators typically use books and other print resources to convey information on the topic. These may include novels, poems, and dramas in English Language Arts, biographies and historical accounts in Social Studies, information about the natural world in Science, and story problems in Mathematics. *Figure 4* shows an example of a math story that embeds pictures in the text to promote student understanding:

Figure 4. Teaching to Standards Math page.

Science information can also be presented in simple summaries with illustrations. Sometimes the chapter in the general education will have a chapter summary that can be used with students who need condensed information. This information can be supplemented with objects and pictures related to the content. *Figure 5* is an excerpt from a science curriculum Attainment Company, Inc., provides.

Figure 5. Teaching to Standards Science page.

Figure 6. From Attainment Company.

To employ literature, children's picture books may be used by adding comprehension questions and response card options. *Figure 6* shows how a response page was adapted in **Building with Stories**.

When using novels, the chapters may need to be rewritten in simpler forms with picture symbols added for clarity. When adapting books, some of the features to consider include:

- Be sure to start with novels that are grade-appropriate.

- Shorten/rewrite the novel using considerate text (e.g., grade 2-3 listening comprehension level).

- Add picture symbols for the main characters and key places and themes that can be used also in comprehension questions; for some students these may be objects that are placed on the page of the book.

- Add definitions and explanations to the text (i.e., "assemble" is a vocabulary word used in **Cheaper by the Dozen**; a line in the adapted text could give meaning to the vocabulary word—"assemble" means to get together).

- A repeated story line that summarizes the main idea of the chapter or book; these can be added to each page.

- Highlighted text for the student to read.

- Physically alter the book to meet the needs of the students (e.g., put the pages of the books in sheet protectors; add page separators to make the pages easier to turn).

Figure 7 is an example of a page of the adapted novel **Cheaper by the Dozen**, created by the General Curriculum Access project at the University of North Carolina at Charlotte.[18]

Figure 7. From the General Curriculum Access Project at UNCC.

[18] http://coedpages.uncc.edu/access/

Selecting Manipulatives

Students with severe disabilities may especially benefit from having hands-on materials. In science, these may include the materials to be used for the experiment in an inquiry approach. *Figure 8* shows some of the materials used in **Teaching to Standards Science**.

Figure 8. Attainment Company's Science experiment materials.

In English Language Arts, these materials may relate to the themes of the story. For example, in a book about apples, the teacher might have a real apple, applesauce to taste, and scented apple products to smell. In a book about baseball, the teacher might have a baseball cap, ball, and bat. Some students may use these objects to answer comprehension questions.

In mathematics, students often need materials to use when applying the mathematics process. For example, to complete a linear equation, students may use sets of objects or a number line. *Figure 9* shows an example of a number line (part of an equation prompt from **Teaching to Standards Math**).

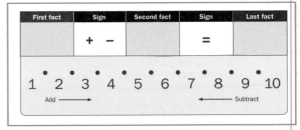

Figure 9. A page from Teaching to Standards Math.

Evidence-Based Teaching Practices

Comprehensive reviews of research provide teachers with effective strategies for teaching academic content.[19] These strategies include the following:

1. **Define the target response the student will make to show learning**. These can either be discrete responses or a chain of responses the student learns to make. The following provide examples.

    a. Discrete responses

        i. Math: identify the number, select geometric shape, read the price

        ii. ELA: read the vocabulary word, answer comprehension questions

        iii. Science: match science word to picture; make a prediction

[19] Browder, D. M., Spooner, F., Ahlgrim-Browder, D. M., Harris, A. & Wakeman, S. (2008). A meta analysis on teaching mathematics to students with significant cognitive disabilities. Exceptional Children, 74, 407-432. Browder, D. M., Wakeman, S. Y., Spooner, F., Ahlgrim-Delzell, L., & Algozzine, B. (2006). Research on reading instruction for individuals with significant cognitive disabilities. Exceptional Children, 72, 392-408. Courtade, G., Spooner, F., & Browder, D. M. (2007). A review of studies with students with significant cognitive disabilities that link to science standards. Research and Practice in Severe Disabilities, 32, 43-49.

iv. Social Studies: state historical fact; identify states

b. Chained responses (also called Task Analysis)

i. Math: steps to solve a linear equation; steps to count out next dollar amount

ii. ELA: steps to complete a story-based lesson/read aloud

iii. Science: steps to participate in an inquiry lesson

iv. Social Studies: steps to fill in a graphic organizer about a historical event

2. **Select a Method of Systematic Prompting and Reinforcement**. Once the target response is determined, the educators can select a method of prompting. The following provide two options that have especially strong research support for teaching academic content.

a. Time Delay

i. In time delay a single prompt is selected. For example, the teacher may model pointing to the correct response on the response board.

ii. The teacher begins by giving the student the cue to respond, for example, "Point to the word 'boy.' "

iii. In the first teaching trials, the teacher gives an immediate (zero delay) prompt so the student can get the correct response every time with no errors. For example, the teacher points to the word "boy" on the student's response board. The teacher praises the student for making these correct prompted responses. (If the student makes errors, choose a better prompt like physical guidance, or teach the student to imitate the teacher's model.)

iv. After the student has had several opportunities to make the response following the teacher's lead, the teacher *delays* the prompt by a few seconds (e.g., 4 seconds) to see if the student will *anticipate* the correct response. If the student does, the teacher praises correct responses. If the student *waits*, the teacher then gives the prompt and praises the student for responding. If the student *does not wait and makes an error*, the teacher repeats the zero delay trial and reminds the student, "Don't guess. If you are not sure, wait and I will help you."

The Early Literacy Skills Builder uses time delay in teaching sight word vocabulary. Teaching to Standards Mathematics and Teaching to Standards Science use time delay in teaching vocabulary as well. Figure 10 is an example of the script the teacher follows:

b. Least-Intrusive Prompts

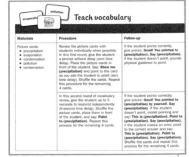

Figure 10

i. The teacher selects a hierarchy of about three prompts. For example, the teacher may decide to use a verbal direction, a model, and physical guidance.

ii. The teacher begins by giving the student the cue to respond. For example, "See what happens when you mix these together" (science experiment). The teacher then waits for the student to take the first step. If the student does (e.g., pours powder in water), the teacher praises and moves to the next step (stirring the water).

iii. If the student does not respond, the teacher gives a verbal direction. "Pour the powder in the water." If the student does, the teacher praises and moves to the next step (stirring).

iv. If the student does not respond, the teacher gives a model. The teacher demonstrates how to pour a bit of the powder in the water and says, "Pour the powder in the water like this. Now you do it." If the student imitates this model, the teacher praises and moves to the next step (stirring).

v. If the student does not respond, the teacher guides the student's hands to make the response while saying, "Here, let me help you pour the powder in the water."

vi. Now the teacher moves to the next step and waits to see if the student will begin to stir the water without prompts. If the student does not, the teacher gives the verbal direction, "Stir the water". . . then demonstrates the model ("stir it like this") . . . and if needed, provides physical guidance. This is repeated for all steps of the task analysis.

3. **Plan the materials, activities, and setting for instruction.**

a. If possible, teach the skill in the general education classroom. For example, you may be able to embed time delay instruction of science terms while other students in the class are working on a science worksheet. Students may be able to do a read aloud of the chapter of a novel with a peer while other students read the text silently.

b. If you will teach the skill in a special education classroom, use the general education teacher as a resource to know what activities and materials are typically used to teach the target skills. For example, it may be helpful to have the science teacher show you a typical experiment to use in teaching the effect of weather on landforms. We have found that students often respond well when this general curriculum content is taught to a small group. Even if students have not been used to group instruction, they may learn the observational and turn-taking skills needed as part of a well organized lesson. These skills will also benefit future inclusive opportunities.

c. There may be commercial resources that will help with planning instruction. The following are some of the resources Attainment offers:

Content Area	Curricula	Age Levels
English Language Arts	Early Literacy Skills Builder Pathways to Literacy Building with Stories *(Coming Soon: Teaching to Standards English/ Language Arts)*	Elementary Middle/High School
Mathematics	*(Coming Soon: Early Math Skills Builder)* Teaching to Standards Math	Elementary Middle/High School
Science	Early Science Teaching to Standards Science Exploring Science Series	Elementary Middle/High School
Social Studies	Explore American History Access American & World History Read for Content: Social Studies	Middle/High School

Formulas for Teaching Content Areas

We have found it helpful to apply some formulas for teaching each content area. There may be other components you will want to add to your lessons but these can get you started.

Formula for Teaching English Language Arts Standards
Read Aloud Text + Vocabulary + Comprehension Questions + Application (e.g., Writing) = ELA Lesson

1. **Read Aloud Text**. To plan the ELA lesson, first select the specific story, poem, drama, or informational text to be read aloud. This should be selected from the student's grade-level literature and adapted as needed for the student's understanding level. For example, in adapting a high school novel, the teacher may write a simple summary of each chapter, add some pictures for the characters and events, and a repeated story line for the main theme of the chapter that is typed on each page. If the student is a reader, the student will read this text aloud. Otherwise, the teacher or a peer can conduct the reading, or assistive technology may be used by the student to play the text aloud. It may be helpful to use a task analysis of the steps the student will follow to interact with the text in this read aloud. For example, the student may find the title and author, turn the pages, read repeated story lines, find key vocabulary, and answer questions as the book is read aloud. To motivate the student for the ELA lesson, the teacher may also introduce the topic of the text using some type of multisensory experience to engage the students. For example, in a text about the ocean, the teacher may play the sounds of waves crashing on the shore, or the songs of whales, and have the students taste "sea water" (salty water).

2. **Teach Key Vocabulary**. The teacher may lead into the story by teaching key vocabulary using a procedure like time delay. This vocabulary may include key character names, frequently occurring sight words, or themes.

3. **Ask Comprehension Questions**. Plan some comprehension questions for the read aloud. For some students these may only require immediate recall. You may even have objects affixed to the page that the student uses to answer the question. Or you may use a response board. As students develop and grow older, use the state standards to plan this comprehension work. For example, an older student may be identifying a story as real or not real, or a simile as real or just an expression.

4. **Teach a Writing Skill**. After the story, the student can engage with the theme of the story by working on a writing standard (e.g., stating an opinion). For some students, "writing" may involve selecting a picture or object to dictate to a scribe how to fill in a sentence (e.g., "My favorite character was . . .") Other IEP goals can also be worked on at this time, like phonics applications or making a presentation to a group.

Formula for Teaching Mathematics Standards

Math Story Read Aloud + Manipulatives + Graphic Organizer + Task Analysis = Math Lesson

1. **Math Story for Read Aloud**. Begin by creating a math story for the math standard to be addressed. These may be adapted from word problems in the general math textbook or created based on activities the students knows and likes. For example, the story may focus on purchasing a pizza, going to the movies, or competing in track and field. The story is written as a simple paragraph. Over days, the specific numbers in the stories can change, so the student does not simply memorize the answer. The stories can also change.

2. **Select Manipulatives**. Students will need manipulatives to "see" what the numbers represent. For example, if there are 2 girls and 3 boys going swimming in the story, the teacher may use pictures as manipulatives or miniature (doll) bathing suits. If the focus is fractions, the teacher may have models of pizzas. Often it is helpful to have a number line with numbers velcroed on it. The students can use the number line to count up or down, to add/subtract, or to pull off a number to express the answer.

3. **Graphic Organizer**. The student may also need a graphic organizer to keep track of the steps required to solve the problem. For example, the student may need a circle for the girls, a circle for the boys, and a "Pool" to put them all in to find the total.

4. **Task Analysis**. The teacher also needs a task analysis of the steps the student will follow to apply the mathematical process (e.g., steps to solve an equation, or steps to plot points on a plane). To develop this, the teacher can consider each response needed to perform the mathematical process using the manipulatives and graphic organizer for support as needed.

5. **Other**. Students may benefit from some time delay instruction to teach mathematics terms like "perimeter" or number recognition. Students may also benefit from practice with math software or the use of a calculator for computation.

Formula for Teaching Science Standards
Science Concept + Science Vocabulary + Science Experiment + Task Analysis/ Inquiry + Response Boards = Science Lesson

1. **Science Concept.** Focus the science lesson on a specific science concept statement. Once the student has discovered the concept through the experiment, the teacher can help the student learn an explanation for the phenomenon. For example: **Some mixtures have a chemical reaction**.

2. **Science Vocabulary.** Students often do not know the terms that will be needed to identify and describe science phenomena. The teacher may begin by using time delay to teach students to match science terms with pictures. Example: vocabulary words (solute, solvent, solution, chemical reaction).

3. **Science Experiment.** Identify an experiment that will help to explain the concept. Example: Mixing solutes (e.g., flour, salt, baking soda) and a solvent (e.g., vinegar) to determine if chemical reactions occur.

4. **Task Analysis/Inquiry Approach.** Rather than simply telling the student the point of the lesson, let the student discover the science concept through a hands-on approach. Frame the inquiry lesson in a task analysis.

The steps of an inquiry lesson are as follows, along with the specific examples for a lesson:

Steps of an Inquiry Lesson	Example-Chemical Reactions[20]
Engage 1. Show students materials	Show students flour, salt, baking soda, and vinegar
2. Ask, "What is it?" *Track student answers on a KWHL chart	Is it sand? Is it salt? Is it a liquid?
3. Ask, "What do you know (K) about the materials?"	Are they wet? Are they dry?
4. Ask, "What do you want (W) to know about the materials?"	What will happen when we mix them together?
Investigate & Describe Relationships 5. Ask, "How (H) can we find out?"	We can mix them together; we can observe them
6. Prediction – Ask students to predict what will happen to the materials after they decide what they will "do" to them	Do you think the solutes will have the same reaction when they are mixed with the solvent (vinegar)? Yes or no?
7. Experiment – Conduct an experiment with the material	Mix each dry material (solute) with the vinegar (solvent) (point out the baking soda bubbling)
8. Ask the students what is the same about the materials before and after the experiment	All are liquids and solutions
9. Ask the students what is different about the materials before and after the experiment	One had a bubbly reaction
Construct Explanation 10. Scientific discovery statement. Use time delay procedure to teach words related to the concept statement and teach students concept statement for that lesson	Vocabulary – solute, solvent, solution, chemical reaction, scientific discovery statement. Some mixtures have a chemical reaction
Report Findings 11. As students, "What did we find out?" and "Why?"	Did all of the solutes have a chemical reaction when we mixed them in the solvent? Yes or no? Why did the mixture in one cup bubble? (It had a chemical reaction.)
12. Ask students, "What did you learn (L)?"	What can happen when you mix materials? Some mixtures have a _____ (chemical reaction).

5. **Response boards**. An inquiry-based science lesson requires a lot of communication. Be sure to include response boards with pictures/objects so that each of your students can be active participants in all steps of the lesson.

[20] Adapted from Courtade, G., Jimenez, B., Trela, K., & Browder, D. M. (2008). *Teaching to standards: Science*. Verona, WI: Attainment Company, Inc.

Creating a Method for Progress Monitoring

Progress monitoring is a crucial component in teaching all students. Teachers must monitor progress in order to determine if students are mastering the skills they are being taught, where any errors are occurring, and what instructional changes should be made. The following are ideas for assessing students with severe disabilities.

- Use task analytic assessment. Task analytic assessment can be used to determine which steps of a task the students were able to complete correctly and which steps the students needed prompting to complete. Following are examples of task analytic assessment forms.

Task Analytic Assessment for a Story-Based Lesson	
The student will:	**Student response:**
1. Interact with materials used during the anticipatory set	
2. Identify vocabulary words	
3. Make a prediction about the story	
4. Identify the title	
5. Identify the author's name	
6. Start the story by opening the book	
7. Turn the page when the teacher or a peer pauses at the end of the page	
8. Find the Table of Contents (HS only)	
9. Identify current chapter (HS only)	
10. Read the repeated story line	
11. Find vocabulary word/ picture on page	
12. Text point to chosen line or page in own book	
13. Answer comprehension questions/review prediction	
2 = completed step independently 1 = completed step with a prompt 0 = did not complete step	

Task Analytic Assessment for Inquiry Science Lesson		
The student will:	Code	Notes/Answers given
1. Explore science materials (touch, look at, etc.)		
2. Answer the question, "What is it?"		
3. Answer the question "What do you know?"		
4. Answer the question "What do you want to know?"		
5. Answer the question "How can we find out?"		
6. Make a prediction by answering the question "What do you think will happen in the experiment?"		
7. Participate in experiment		
8. Answer the question, "What is the same?"		
9. Answer the question, "What is different?"		
10. Read/identify concept statement and identify vocabulary		Concept statement: Vocabulary words:
11. Answer the questions, "What did we find out?" and "Why?"		
12. Answer the question, "What did we learn?"		
2 = completed step independently 1 = completed step with a prompt 0 = did not complete step		

Task Analytic Assessment for a Math Lesson (ex: Algebra)		
The student will:	**Code**	**Notes**
Identify math terms/vocabulary		Terms/vocabulary:
Identify the problem		
Identify all facts in the story 1st fact: 2nd fact: Last fact:		
Place chips on number line		
Identify the operation to use		
Count using the number line		
Solve for x		
Restate the problem statement		
State the solution in the story context		
2 = completed step independently 1 = completed step with a prompt 0 = did not complete step		

- Use discrete trial (repeated trial) assessment. Discrete trial assessment can be used to determine if students are mastering discrete skills such as identifying vocabulary words or concept statements. The following examples are two data sheets that could be used to track acquisition of science vocabulary and concepts (first data sheet) sheet and identification of the numbers 1-10 (second data sheet).

Progress monitoring form

Student's name **Lilliana** Date **6/8-6/14**

Unit: ☐ Earth ☑ Biology ☐ Waters ☐ Chemistry   Lesson **3**

Key: − error   + independent correct   M model/prompt

Dates	6/8	6/9	6/10	6/13	6/14
Picture cards					
cell	M	M	+	+	
cell division	M	M	+	+	
bacteria	M	M	+	+	
disease	M	M	M	+	
nutrition	M	M	M	M	
Word cards					
cell	M	M	+	+	
cell division	M	M	+	+	
bacteria	M	M	M	+	
disease	M	M	M	+	
nutrition	M	M	M	M	
Picture/word card match					
cell	M	M	M	+	
cell division	M	M	M	+	
bacteria	M	M	M	M	
disease	M	M	M	M	
nutrition	M	M	M	M	
Concept statement:					
Cell division makes living things grow.	−	−	−	+	

Student:					Skill: The student will identify numbers 1-10 by pointing to each number when requested (4 of 5 trials correct)					
Dates:										
1										
2										
3										
4										
5										
6										
7										
8										
9										
10										
Total Independent Correct:										

Student response code:

I = independent

V = verbal prompt

M = model prompt

P = physical prompt

- Make data-based decisions
  Once data has been collected, it is important to use the data both to measure progress, and to make instructional changes. One way to determine if a student is making adequate progress to meet an IEP goal is to graph the data on a line graph using a progress line that reflects the current trend of the student data, and an aimline that reflects where the student data should be if the student is to master the skill in a given amount of time. For example, if a goal for a student is to be able to identify numbers 1-10 by the end of December, a graph with student data may look like this:

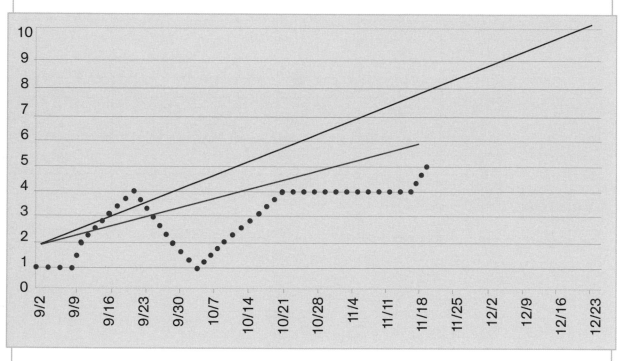

This graph shows the trend of the current student data (data points and trend line - green line) and also an aimline (red line) of where the student's progress should be if the student is to master this goal by the end of December. As you can see, the student data is consistently falling below the aimline. This indicates that the student is not on track for mastery by December. If a student's data indicates that he/she is not on track for mastery, instructional changes need to occur. The following are some general guidelines and examples for making data-based decisions:

What does the student data look like?	Potential Solutions
Student data points are consistently above the aimline	The student will master this goal early. Continue your current instruction. When the student masters the goal, challenge the student by writing another goal that is more difficult.
Student data points are consistent with the aimline	The student is on track for mastery. Do not change instruction.

Student data points are consistently below the aimline

Potential Problem (Check which applies)	Potential Solutions
Learning Problems	
_____ 1. Skill is too difficult. (e.g., There have been no unprompted responses in at least a month of instruction.)	Plan how to simplify response (i.e. task analyze the skill) or use assistive technology to make skill achievable.
_____ 2. Student is making progress, but it is too slow for mastery to occur this IEP year.	Plan ways to fade prompting more systematically. Schedule more training trials for each day.
_____ 3. Student's performance has regressed or is highly variable (not due to medical problems or overall behavioral problems).	Increase motivation by using varied and highly preferred reinforcers. Enhance natural consequences. Ignore errors.
Programming Problems	
_____ 1. Student performance has regressed across all or most skills.	Discuss medical/behavioral interventions needed.
_____ 2. Data not collected reliably. Skill not taught consistently.	Review and plan for needed staff training or time management.

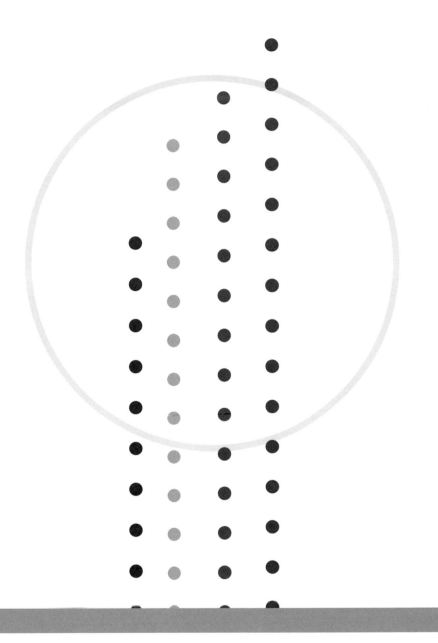

Appendix

Attainment Overlays/GoTalk:

Attainment Company Inc. produces cost-effective, age-appropriate learning and AT products for children and adults with special needs. For more information contact:

Attainment Company, Inc.
504 Commerce Parkway
Verona, WI 53593-0160
1-800-327-4269
www.AttainmentCompany.com

IntelliKeys Keyboard:

Intellitools' mission is to provide outstanding technology to help all students learn to their fullest potential. For more information contact:

Intellitools, Inc.
1720 Corporate Circle
Petaluma CA 94954
1-800-899-6687
www.intellitools.com

Power Link:

AbleNet, Inc., is dedicated to making a difference in the lives of people with disabilities by creating products and ideas that make teaching students easy, fun, and fulfilling. For more information contact:

AbleNet
2808 Fairview Avenue
Roseville, MN 55113-1308
1-800-322-0956 US and Canada
www.ablenetinc.com

Automatic Pourer:

Enabling Devices is a company dedicated to developing affordable learning and assistive devices to help people of all ages with disabling conditions. For more information contact:

Enabling Devices
385 Warburton Avenue
Hastings on Hudson, NY 10502
1-800-832-8697
www.enablingdevices.com

RJ's MP3 Player-Drive:

RJ Cooper & Associates is a company that creates special software and hardware for products for persons with special needs. For more information contact:

RJ Cooper & Associates
27601 Forbes Rd. Suite 39
Laguna Niguel, CA 92677
http://www.rjcooper.com/index.html
1-800-RJCooper

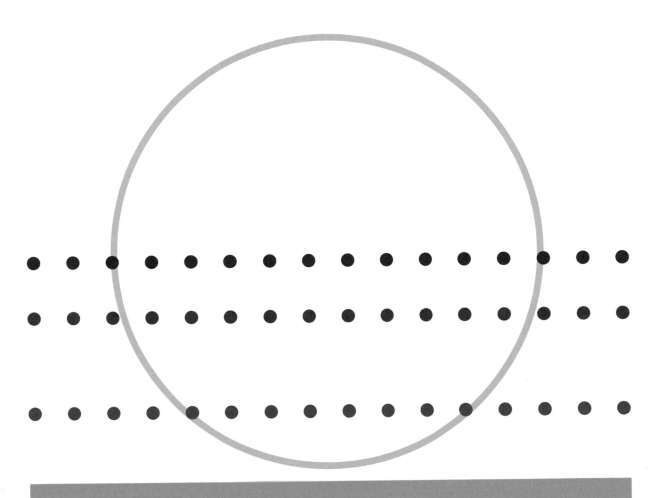

Notes

1 http://www.corestandards.org/the-standards/english-language-arts-standards/writing/grade-4/

2 Individuals with Disabilities Education Improvement Act of 2004, 20 U. S. C. §1400, H. R. 1350.

3 No Child Left Behind Act of 2001, Pub. L. No. 107-110, 115 Stat.1425 (2002).

4 http://www.govtrack.us/congress/bill.xpd?bill=s111-2781

5 Example abstracted from the Resource Guide to the Massachusetts Curriculum Frameworks for Students with Disabilities: Science and Technology/ Engineering published by the Massachusetts Department of Education http://www.doe.mass.edu/mcas/alt/rg/sci.pdf pp. 260-261.

6 http://www.cde.state.co.us/cdeassess/UAS/CoAcademicStandards.html

7 http://www.corestandards.org/the-standards/english-language-arts-standards/reading-literature-6-12/grade-7/

8 This information on writing IEP objectives is adapted from Bateman and Herr, Writing Measurable IEP Goals and Objectives, Attainment Company/IEP Resources Publication (2003).

9 http://www.corestandards.org/the-standards/english-language-arts-standards/introduction/how-to-read-the-standards/

10 Towles-Reeves, E., Kleinert, H., & Muhomba, M. (2009). Alternate assessment: Have we learned anything new? Exceptional Children, 75, 233-252.

11 http://www.corestandards.org/the-standards/english-language-arts-standards

12 http://www.corestandards.org/the-standards/mathematics/introduction/standards-for-mathematical-practice/

13 http://www.corestandards.org/the-standards/mathematics

14 http://www.corestandards.org/the-standards/mathematics

15 http://www.corestandards.org/the-standards/mathematics/high-school-modeling/introduction/

16 http://www.corestandards.org/the-standards/mathematics

17 Find virtual manipulatives at http://nlvm.usu.edu/en/nav/vlibrary.html

18 http://coedpages.uncc.edu/access/

19 Browder, D. M., Spooner, F., Ahlgrim-Browder, D. M., Harris, A., & Wakeman, S. (2008). A meta-analysis on teaching mathematics to students with significant cognitive disabilities. *Exceptional Children*, 74, 407-432.

Browder, D. M., Wakeman, S. Y., Spooner, F., Ahlgrim-Delzell, L., & Algozzine, B. (2006). Research on reading instruction for individuals with significant cognitive disabilities. *Exceptional Children*, 72, 392-408.

Courtade, G., Spooner, F., & Browder, D. M. (2007). A review of studies with students with significant cognitive disabilities that link to science standards. *Research and Practice in Severe Disabilities*, 32, 43-49.

20 Adapted from Courtade, G., Jimenez, B., Trela, K., & Browder, D. M. (2008). *Teaching to standards: Science*. Verona, WI: Attainment Company, Inc.

New book to come

Instructional Tools for Teaching Standards-Based IEPs

By Bree Jimenez PhD, Ginevra Courtade, PhD, and Diane M. Browder, PhD

Instructional Tools for Teaching Standards-Based IEPs is designed to provide educators with specific strategies, techniques, and formulas to provide students with the instruction needed to successful master IEP goals. This resource guides educators to teach to standards-based IEPs using research and evidence based practices. Case studies and planning forms will be included.